Writing Science Right

Help your students improve their science understanding and communicate their knowledge more effectively. *Writing Science Right* shows you the best ways to teach content-area writing so that students can share their learning and discoveries through informal and formal writing assignments and oral presentations.

You'll teach students how to . . .

♦ identify their audience and an appropriate organizational structure for their writing;
♦ achieve a readable style by knowing the reader's background knowledge;
♦ build effective sentences and concise paragraphs;
♦ prepare and deliver oral presentations that bring content to life;
♦ use major science articles, abstracts, and summaries as mentor texts;
♦ and more!

Throughout the book, you'll find a wide variety of sample articles and suggested assignments that you can use immediately. In addition, a list of additional teaching texts and resources is available on the Routledge website at www.routledge.com/9781138302679.

Sue Neuen has had 16 years' experience as a school administrator and teacher. She received a Master of Science degree in Educational Administration with emphasis on School Restructuring from the University of Wisconsin–Madison, WI.

Elizabeth Tebeaux, Professor Emerita, has 35 years in English at Texas A&M. She received her PhD from A&M, her MA in English from Sam Houston State University, a MEd from the University of Houston, and a BA from Baylor University in Math and English.

Other Eye On Education Books
Available from Routledge
(www.routledge.com/eyeoneducation)

DIY Project Based Learning for Math and Science
Heather Wolpert-Gawron

DIY Project Based Learning for ELA and History
Heather Wolpert-Gawron

STEM by Design:
Strategies and Activities for Grades 4–8
Anne Jolly

The STEM Coaching Handbook:
Working with Teachers to Improve Instruction
Terry Talley

History Class Revisited:
Tools and Projects to Engage Middle School Students in Social Studies
Jody Passanisi

Judging for Themselves:
Using Mock Trials to Bring Social Studies and English to Life
David Sherrin

The Classes They Remember:
Using Role-Plays to Bring Social Studies and English to Life
David Sherrin

Writing Strategies That Work:
Do This—Not That!
Lori G. Wilfong

The Multimedia Writing Toolkit:
Helping Students Incorporate Graphics and Videos for Authentic
Purposes, Grades 3–8
Sean Ruday

Rigor Is NOT a Four-Letter Word, Second Edition
Barbara R. Blackburn

Writing Science Right

Strategies for Teaching Scientific and Technical Writing

Sue Neuen and Elizabeth Tebeaux

Routledge
Taylor & Francis Group

NEW YORK AND LONDON

First published 2018
by Routledge
711 Third Avenue, New York, NY 10017

and by Routledge
2 Park Square, Milton Park, Abingdon, Oxon, OX14 4RN

Routledge is an imprint of the Taylor & Francis Group, an informa business

Library of Congress Cataloging-in-Publication Data
A catalog record for this book has been requested

ISBN: 978-1-138-30266-2 (hbk)
ISBN: 978-1-138-30267-9 (pbk)
ISBN: 978-1-315-17857-8 (ebk)

Typeset in Palatino
by Apex CoVantage, LLC

Visit the eResources: www.routledge.com/9781138302679

Contents

eResources

This book contains mentor texts throughout—science abstracts, articles, and more. An updated list of additional resources will be available online. In addition, the full PowerPoint presentations from Chapter 4 will be available online. To access these materials, go to the book website at www.routledge.com/9781138302679 and click on the tab that says "eResources."

Meet the Authors

Sue Neuen served as Executive Director of Science@OC from 2003 to 2016, carrying out the mission to inspire secondary school students in Orange County, California, to excel in science and explore STEM (Science, Technology, Engineering, and Mathematics) careers so they are capable of competing for college placement and positioned for future STEM careers. Science@OC partners with educators to develop strategic plans to implement inquiry-based science programs, foster leadership, provide effective professional development, and engage the community to support STEM education. Under her leadership, Science@OC grew to impact one third of the 113,700 middle school students in science programs in Orange County. During her tenure, Sue founded the STEMCorps that connects Educators and STEM Professionals to enhance the teaching and learning of STEM through Project-based Learning collaborations and "real-world" connections.

As a LASER (Leadership and Assistance for Science Education Reform) faculty member, a program of the *Smithsonian Science Education Center* of the Smithsonian Institution, Sue has facilitated district level strategic planning for K–12 science programs across the United States. She served on the National Alliance for State Science and Math Coalitions (NASSMC) Board of Directors. She is an international speaker (Mexico, Chile, Canada, Netherlands, Poland, and Australia) on "Global Competitiveness, STEM Education and the 21st Century Workforce Preparedness." Sue is secretary for MANCEF, the Micro, Nano, and Emerging Technologies Commercialization Education Foundation.

Before coming to California, Sue served as the Director of The Einstein Project in Green Bay, Wisconsin, from 1995 to 2002. In her tenure there, she brought the Einstein Project through the transition from a small nine-district program to a successful, nationally recognized non-profit organization providing Science Education Services to over 70 school districts.

Sue has had 16 years' experience as a school administrator and teacher. She received a Master of Science degree in Educational Administration with emphasis on School Restructuring from the University of Wisconsin–Madison, WI.

Elizabeth (Beth) Tebeaux served as Professor of English at Texas A&M University (TAMU) from 1980 to 2016. She currently has Emeritus status at the University. Beth created the technical communication program at TAMU, grew the service course enrollment from 450 to 3,600 students per year in just eight years, and developed the first Writing Specialization to prepare technical writers. She has written seven technical writing college texts. In addition, Beth developed composition and technical communication teachers for TAMU and the first MBA communication courses and writing courses for the Professional Accounting Program.

Beth launched the Office of Distance Education at TAMU at the request of the TAMU Provost, working with colleges and departments to develop and launch 25 graduate programs and three graduate certificate programs from 1998 to 2006. She became first faculty member at TAMU to teach via the World Wide Web and at Rice, for which she developed all procedures and policies governing distance education at TAMU, which included writing the *Guide to Distance Education at TAMU*.

Beth developed and taught a wide range of courses in applied communication for graduate and undergraduate students at both Rice and TAMU. She redesigned and taught Writing for Publication for graduate students in a variety of disciplines, specifically targeting non-English–speaking students. She was the principal co-founder of *Explorations*, A&Ms' undergraduate journal.

Beth was the first technical communication faculty member to win an Andrew Mellon Fellowship for research at The Huntington Library after writing the history of technical writing in the English Renaissance and a second book on history of technical writing in England in the 17th century.

Beth has 35 years in English at Texas A&M. She received her PhD from A&M, her MA in English from Sam Houston State University, a MEd from the University of Houston, and a BA from Baylor University in Math and English.

Preface

Writing Science Right targets the four Cs (Creativity, Critical Thinking, Collaboration, and Communication) outlined in the *Framework for 21st Century Learning*. The document was developed by teachers, experts in education, and leaders in business to define the skills and knowledge students need for the 21st century. Today, skills take center stage when it comes to teaching and learning, and teachers need tools to help them succeed. We believe that *Writing Science Right* provides that tool.

In this fast-paced technological age, clear, concise transfer of information has become more important than ever. Students need to verbalize their knowledge and understanding through writing and oral presentations. Mastering these skills has become particularly critical in the fields of STEM (Science, Technology, Engineering, and Mathematics) because STEM-focused jobs now significantly out-pace non-STEM jobs.

Today's teachers must help students begin early to develop skills to communicate their thinking in an organized, audience-specific way. They need to know how to prioritize knowledge to be transferred, the best format or media to use, and the level at which their audience would like to receive the information.

By the end of World War II, knowledge was doubling every 25 years. Today, nanotechnology knowledge doubles every two years; clinical knowledge, every 18 months. However, on average, human knowledge doubles only every 13 months.

This book provides teachers with the necessary tools to help their students communicate their discoveries, understanding, and knowledge like real scientists and engineers. In addition, this book supplies teachers with exemplary resources to guide students through STEM education pathways where *Writing Science Right* will impact their future opportunities.

We offer this book for three major reasons:

1) English Language Arts and Science have each been taught in silos, not as cross-discipline topics. Secondary school writing instruction hardly exists, and students lack exposure to rhetorical principles: how to write to your readers, how to ensure that readers want to read what you write, and how to effectively give an oral presentation. *Writing Science Right* fills a serious need in both secondary science and English Language Arts education.

2) As authors, each of us has an established reputation in our fields: science education and technical communication. We believe that writing needs to be presented as technical writing, and science education needs to be more relevant and rigorous than it is or has been. Cross-discipline learning, not a new concept, can enrich both science and writing instruction for all secondary school students.

3) Writing instruction has for years been taught as essay writing—with the teacher as the only audience. Essays have limited value, as workforce writing requires a variety of skills to communicate to various audiences. Teachers need to know and be able to teach their students about different levels of science communication.

In short, we prepare Writing Science Right *as a resource for teachers to provide a rich supplement to standard, state-approved texts that offer science as a stand-alone topic and often lack methods for communicating the meaning of science. Students can develop those skills in research projects.*

Teacher understanding of technical writing for science and effectiveness of student writing has continued to weaken during the last half century. Educators continue to stress basic elements of writing, culminating in essays that have no rhetorical situation. In short, in elementary and secondary school contexts, writing exists for itself. Students are burdened with grades on themes and essays about topics that lack relevance in their daily lives. To help teachers motivate and educate students, *Writing Science Right* provides resources to illustrate important, current, and relevant topics, such as diseases (Zika, malaria, West Nile virus, Ebola, and antibiotic-resistant tuberculosis) that have moved into the United States and have severe impact on populations of all ages. We want students to recognize that major issues, such as those just mentioned, affect them as students, as future employees (hopefully scientists and engineers), and as maturing adults.

Writing Science Right will provide an up-to-date reference list on the Taylor & Francis website for teacher use on the issues we present (see www.taylorand francis.com/9781138302679). All references can serve as the foundation for future teacher-created assignments so that teachers do not have to rely on "old" topics and assignments found in traditional textbooks.

To the Teacher: How to Use *Writing Science Right*

As a teacher of science, you have a unique responsibility to spark curiosity in students so that they want to better understand their world. Motivating students to "want to learn more" provides one of the biggest challenges teachers face. Micro and nanotechnology permeate all the disciplines. Instruction in isolated silos has become a remnant of the past. The 21st century has become an exciting time to teach science! *Writing Science Right*, with its current and relevant topics along with references to keep topics updated, provides you with ammunition to motivate any student.

Writing Science Right has been structured to first inform you, the teacher, on basic technical writing guidelines set for students at Texas A&M, a research university, and other institutions of higher learning. After you have become familiar with these guidelines, we hope that you will help students implement them through the assignments provided.

Writing Science Right *fills a gap in science instruction: how to write about science. No basic instruction currently exists for good technical writing at the middle school or early high school levels. We use many articles focused on current diseases which have become a major issue; diseases no longer remain in one country. They move swiftly, as carriers of diseases can fly across the world in a matter of days, bringing potential death or deformity to those who get the disease. The concept of One Health illuminates the merging of veterinary medicine and human medicine as disease no longer is limited to just humans or animals.*

Writing Science Right is not designed to be a stand-alone curriculum but a small book designed for integration into your current teaching assignments. As you prepare your lessons, identify ways in which you can enhance students' learning and abilities in writing and presenting findings. We provide examples and articles for you as you move through the chapters. We suggest you read the whole book first and then decide how you will integrate technical writing into your instruction. You will find that many articles focus on health issues, diseases, and epidemics, which serve two purposes: one, to educate and inform the students and, two, to see what good examples of science writing and research looks like. We hope you will share the articles and letters from the book with your students.

We also provide you with assignments to use directly with your students or to serve as examples to assist you in creating your own assignments to complement the science content you are covering. Many assignments are not individualized but have your students working in pairs or groups, emulating today's workplace environment.

Thank you for choosing to prepare your students in *Writing Science Right*. Your students will thank you. And don't be surprised if your colleagues thank you as student writing improves in all areas of their education.

Synopsis

Writing Science Right will cover the basics of technical writing: knowing your audience and purpose; practicing clear and effective writing; presenting findings in formats such as memo reports and science letters, a genre common to most science magazines and journals, and the short science/technical reports common to research and industry; and components of an effective oral presentation, including basic visuals, such as effective PowerPoint presentations. Chapters 1, 2 and 4 focus on the basics of technical writing and presentations. Chapters 3 and 5 "teach" these principles via short letters and major science reports, which become the foundation for technical writing assignments. They invite students to discuss short articles from major science/medical journals such as *The Lancet*, a well-established, highly respected medical science journal that deals with current issues in One Health science.

We anticipate routine refreshment of resources on the book website, which will allow rapid replacement of science articles from which teachers can develop student assignments. We encourage teachers to develop websites that allow them to develop their own place to illustrate sources they find and want to share with students.

1

Writing for the Readers: Know Your Audience and Analyze Their Needs

What Is Writing Science Anyway?

Writing science—to explain, describe, argue for or against scientific ideas—differs from other writing students have done in school. All of us learn to write by writing to our teachers. Our goal: to get a good grade, which we hope shows that we understand the material that has been presented. However, as we begin to study science and do so with more depth, we have to recognize that if we *Write Science Right*, we have to learn to write to a variety of readers, depending on the purpose we have in writing and the knowledge level of our audience.

The foundation of writing science and any technical writing is knowing how to write for its readers. This chapter will explain how to help your students design basic reports for various readers.

To begin:

1. Readers must understand the meaning of what is written exactly as the writer intended.
2. Writing must achieve its goal with the reader.
3. Writers must create and maintain a positive relationship with their readers.

Questions for students to ask themselves about their readers:

◆ Who will read what I write?
◆ How much do they know about my topic?

- ◆ What is their educational background?
- ◆ Will they be interested in what I write?
- ◆ Why am I writing? What do I want them to know or do from what I have written?

All writing is not the same and differs based on readers, purpose, context, and the subject.

Figure 1.1

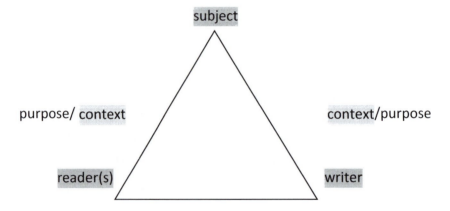

All communication occurs in a context, the area outside the triangle in Figure 1.1. The subject, purpose, writer, and readers occur as a result of the context—what is occurring that makes the communication necessary. The emphasis and relationship among the three will determine the communication type.

For example, *in science writing*, the writer wants to create a relationship between the **subject** and the **reader(s).** The writer must attempt to bring the readers to the subject by knowing the readers' needs and the intended goal for writing.

Communication forms assume their character depending on the relationships established around the communication triangle between the writer, the reader, and the subject.

Figure 1.2

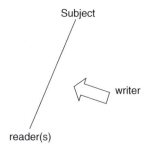

If the writer wants to establish a specific relationship with the reader through his writing, the result will be expository writing, such as news articles, or essays.

If the writer wants to address the subject, the result can be literature.

writer _____ subject.

Helping Students Create and Organize Their Writing
1. Collecting and Grouping Information
2. Planning Content Development According to Four Reader-Friendly Text Patterns:
   A. Topical Arrangement
   B. Reports Designed for Specific Reader Needs
   C. Chronological Arrangement
   D. Persuasive Argument Arrangement
3. Strategies for Developing Content
   A. Partitions
   B. Definitions
   C. Questions
   D. Headings

When developing a report, first be sure students know the subject. They should not just begin writing! During the process of collecting information from research, interviews, and assimilation of material about the topic, have them think about how to organize the information collected: ways to arrange the ideas, where to place material within specific sections, how to decide "what goes where." Considering arrangement of content during planning helps generate content in collecting information.

> Organization is the heart and soul of effective writing.

Collecting and Grouping Information

During research for information, have your students try grouping material and notes into specific categories. Have them label the categories. Next, instruct them to consider developing the report around main sections—the introduction and then information categories ordered in terms of the report purpose and reader needs. For long reports, students should consider having a file for each section, starting with the introduction.

Introduction

State the purpose of the report—what the report expects to accomplish and what reader(s) should learn. Any additional information can be included later. Stating the report purpose at the beginning of the draft helps students stay focused and tells reader(s) what to expect. Students can initially write down a list of the categories or topics that will be covered to achieve the purpose of the report:

Category/topic 1: phrase describing the issue you want to present
Category/topic 2: etc.
Category/topic 3: etc.

Figure 1.3

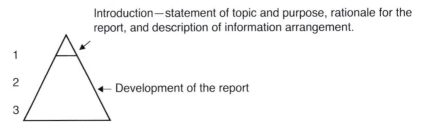

Introduction—statement of topic and purpose, rationale for the report, and description of information arrangement.

← Development of the report

After your students have determined the report information categories, they can begin inserting information under each topic or subject category. Initially, they insert information under the appropriate general topic. They can combine, revise, and delete ideas later. Examine the three paragraphs taken from James Watson's *DNA: The Secret of Life*, Example 1.1. Watson carefully designs these paragraphs to help readers follow the DNA story. Note how Watson begins with a direct topic sentence (underlined), and then he develops support for the topic sentence. The more complex the concept is, the more important it is to carefully develop and organize the paragraphs to allow readers to follow the author's main idea.

Notice how Watson uses *examples* to explain DNA in this first paragraph. As we will show, examples, description, and cause/effect provide just a few of the ways to explain concepts.

Example 1.1: Organizing Information Under Topics

¶ 1. The human body is bewilderingly complex. Traditionally, biologists have focused on one small part and tried to understand it in detail. This basic approach did not change with the advent of molecular biology. Scientists for the most part still specialize on one gene or on the genes involved in one biochemical pathway. But the parts of any machine do not operate independently. If I were to study the carburetor of my car engine, even in exquisite detail, I would still have no idea about the overall function of the engine, much less the entire car. To understand what an engine is for, and how it works, I'd need to study the whole thing—I'd need to place the carburetor in context, as one functioning part among many. The same is true of genes. To understand the genetic processes underpinning life, we need more than a detailed knowledge of particular genes or pathways; we need to place that knowledge in the context of the entire system—the genome.

(165)

In the second paragraph, Watson uses *amplification* to give readers a sense of the size of DNA.

¶ 2. The genome is the entire set of genetic instructions in the nucleus of every cell. (In fact, each cell contains two genomes, one derived from each parent: the two copies of each chromosome we inherit furnish us with two copies of each gene, and therefore two copies of the genome.) Genome sizes vary from species to species. From measurement of the amount of DNA in a single cell, we have been able to estimate that the human genome—half the DNA contents of a single nucleus—contains some 3.1 billion base pairs: 3,1000,000,000 As, Ts, Gs, and Cs.

In paragraph 3, Watson provides more examples, this time describing some of the ways genes affect our human lives.

¶ 3. Above all, the human genome contains the key to our humanity. Genes figure in our every success and woe, even the ultimate one: they are implicated to some extent in all causes of mortality except accidents. In the most obvious cases, diseases like cystic fibrosis and Tay-Sachs are caused directly by mutations. But many other genes have work just as deadly, if more oblique, influencing our susceptibility to common killers like cancer and heart disease, both of which may run in families. Even our response to infectious diseases like measles and the common cold has a genetic component since the immune system is governed by our DNA. And aging is largely a genetic phenomenon as well: the effects we associate with getting older are to some extent a reflection of the lifelong accumulation of mutations in our genes. Thus, if we are to understand fully, and ultimately come to grips with, these life-or-death genetic factors, we must have a complete inventory of all genetic players in the human body.

By organizing information, students can watch ideas grow to meet the report purpose. Rearranging topics, paragraphs, and sentences is easier as they work within each section. As they insert information, they can see how a topic or category develops. Thanks to computers, revising and rearranging text is easy and time efficient.

Example 1.2 also follows a triangular pattern in its introduction. The topic sentence sets the stage for the remainder of the paragraph. Have your students list sentences they know they want to include, then have them arrange the sentences. This process will help them develop a topic sentence for each paragraph that provides the overview of all the paragraph's details.

Example 1.2: Another Triangular Pattern

This paper reviews the historical and recent progress in TB control to show what has changed since the introduction of directly observed therapy (DOTS).

The Stop TB Strategy and the Global Plan to Stop TB were launched in 2006 to achieve the tuberculosis (TB)-related Millennium Development Goals and the Stop TB Partnership targets, and to address new challenges such as that of HIV-associated TB and multi-drug-resistant TB.

Major progress was seen in most countries in the last two decades.

Globally, the estimated rates of TB prevalence and mortality are declining, but not quickly enough to reach the 2015 Stop TB Partnership targets of halving TB prevalence and death rates compared with 1990.

In 2007, it was estimated that more than one-third of TB patients were not detected or properly treated under proper conditions.

Enhancing case detection, while maintaining high treatment success rates, is essential to achieve the 2015 targets.

The ultimate goal of TB control is the elimination of the disease as a public health problem.

The Stop TB Partnership aims at eliminating TB by 2050 by reaching a global incidence of disease of less than one case per million population.

This target will not be achieved unless TB control efforts are further intensified and effectively and affordability developed than rapidly introduced in all countries worldwide. New technologies to prevent both disease and infection remain critical.

Planning Content Development

After determining the paragraphs or sections needed, designing the report will depend on (1) the kind of report needed and/or (2) the readers' information needs, as well as (3) the purpose of the report.

Topical Arrangement

In topical arrangement, the order for presenting ideas should be logical and inclusive: The report should supply the information the reader needs. For example, in a report on disease management of citrus fruit, the writer arranges the report by grouping information about specific citrus diseases. He describes, in parallel arrangement, the main diseases (see Example 1.3) in his outline.

Example 1.3: Outline in Topical Arrangement
Introduction—Description of Treatments for Citrus Diseases
Body of Report—Citrus Diseases and Factors in Treating Them

Disease #1—Melanose
- ◆ Description
- ◆ Factors to be considered before the application of fungicides for melanose control
  Table I. Chemical controls for melanose

Disease #2—Greasy Spot
- ◆ Description
- ◆ Factors to be considered in the management of greasy spot
  Table II: Chemical controls for greasy spot

Disease #3—Foot Rot
- ◆ Description
- ◆ Factors to consider in managing the disease
  Table III: Chemical controls for foot rot

Disease #4—Citrus Nematode
- ◆ Description
- ◆ Sampling instructions to determine presence of citrus nematode
  Table IV: Citrus nematode counts considered low, medium or high at
    specific times during the growing season

Conclusion: Factors to Consider Before Applying Nematicides
Table V: Chemical controls for nematodes (Summary)

Once the citrus researcher has arranged his information, he can begin inserting information beneath each topic heading. The parallel arrangement and use of summary tables allows the writer and readers to move quickly through the report and enables readers to compare various citrus diseases. The writer has designed the full report to be easily read by fruit growers who need to be able to diagnose these typical citrus diseases.

Reports Designed for Specific Reader Needs
Depending on what they know of readers' perspective on the topic, students should determine what information needs to be placed first. If their readers will resist what they say, students need to "buffer" critical points with background information that prepares the reader for the main "news." If the reader already wants "the facts," then the report should begin with "the facts."

Topical arrangement is the most common type of arrangement. If some information is of greater importance than other information, place information in descending order of importance, usually, to ensure that the most important information appears first.

List ideas in order of importance.

Example 1.4: Ideas in Order of Importance

In this short news article from *The Lancet* (Volume 387, Issue 10027, p. 1483) about diabetes, a Non-Communicable Disease (NCD), the writer emphasizes the troubling numbers.

Beat Diabetes: An Urgent Call for Global Action

The theme of this year's World Health Day on April 7—Beat diabetes—adds to a 2011 UN initiative to stem the rise in prevalence of diabetes by 2025, as well as to reduce premature deaths from non-communicable diseases, part of Sustainable Development Goal 3. In today's *Lancet*, the NCD Risk-Factor Collaboration (NCD-RisC) report that in 2014, an estimated 422 million people worldwide were living with diabetes—roughly a four-fold increase over the past 35 years. The NCD-RisC pooled data from 751 studies that measured either fasting plasma glucose or haemoglobin A1c to determine global and regional trends in diabetes prevalence. And, as Etienne Krug highlights in an accompanying Comment, these data "sound the alarm for large-scale, effective action". The outlook for some regions is promising, with almost no changes in age-adjusted prevalence reported for both men and women in northwestern and southwestern Europe from 1980 to 2014, remaining below 6% for women and 8% for men. By contrast, in 2014, prevalence was higher than 25% in some islands of Polynesia and Micronesia, and as high as 31% and 33% for men and women, respectively, in American Samoa, which are also regions with high rates of obesity. These divergent statistics clearly show that beating diabetes on a global scale cannot be achieved with a one-size-fits-all approach.

Chronological Arrangement

Some topics can be presented in time order. In this arrangement, your students explain or present information sequentially—in the order in which events occurred. The following outline of a literature review of *Cultural Control of the Boll Weevil—A Four Season Approach—Texas Rolling Plains* illustrates chronological arrangement. This technical report surveys and reviews existing research on how boll weevils can be controlled throughout the agricultural year. Note, too, that the segments use parallel development, and each segment ends with a summary of that segment. This approach allows the reader to choose where to begin and how much to read. For example, the reader may wish to read only the Summary and Introduction and the factual summary for each season. Good technical and scientific writing, through its use of headings and subheadings, allows readers to read all or part of the report.

Example 1.5: Outline in Chronological Arrangement
Cultural Control of the Boll Weevil—A Four Season Approach—Texas Rolling Plains

Table of Contents

- Summary [of the entire report}
- Introduction
- Spring Cultural Control
    - Prepare the land for planting
    - Utilize delayed planting
    - Use uniform planting
    - Summary
- Summer Cultural Control
    - Shorten the growing season
    - Change the microclimate
        - Row direction
        - Bed shape
        - Row spacing
    - Summary
- Fall Cultural Control
    - Utilize harvest-aid chemicals
    - Role of planting date
    - Terminate irrigations in August
    - Summary
- Winter Cultural Control
    - Eliminate the overwintering habitat
    - Modify the overwintering habitat
    - Avoid the overwintering habitat
    - Summary
- Conclusions
- Acknowledgments
- Supporting Research Studies

Persuasive Argument Arrangement

Many times reports argue for a specific point or position. "Argument" means your students need to persuade their readers. Prompting your students to understand what objections will have to be overcome will be critical to report planning and the presentation of arguments. Reports that must produce conclusions and recommendations may require writers to develop conclusions and recommendations that are not what readers will welcome. On the other hand, these reports may be prepared for readers who have no preconceived ideas. In each situation, the report can be designed to anticipate the perspective of the readers.

Strategies for Developing Content

Technical/science writing, in its most basic form, explains, describes, or defines concepts.

Partitions

Students can use several methods to explain a topic: First, they can *partition* the topic or concept to be presented or explained into workable units (as shown in the reports on citrus disease and the four-season approach to boll weevil control). Science writing must be carefully and logically *partitioned* so that readers can follow and understand the content as they move through the report. Please find listed below methods students can use to clearly partition a topic.

- ◆ definitions of terms
- ◆ partition of the topic into units
- ◆ description
- ◆ background of the concept
- ◆ visual and verbal illustrations, analogies
- ◆ examples
- ◆ cause/effect analysis
- ◆ comparison and contrast
- ◆ etymology (the origin and the historical development of a word)
- ◆ history
- ◆ amplification

Definitions

In good technical and science writing, writers use these strategies in building explanation. Look at Example 1.6, which defines an annelid, a roundworm, by developing the descriptive information and using many of the strategies in the list above. Example 1.6 begins with a definition and partitions the term into three divisions: Polychaeta, Oligochaeta, and Hirudinae. The writer then uses other devices to explain each term—comparison/contrast, description, etymology, illustration—to show how each partition relates to the main definition.

Example 1.6: Definition and Partitions of Annelid

The annelid example in Figure 1.4 shows one way writers organize material: 1. Begin with a definition. 2. Partition the term. 3. Develop methods to relate each partition to the other two: Can I compare them? Contrast them? Describe each? Use examples? These methods help shape the information.

Now look at Example 1.7, which describes diverticulosis and illustrates many of the strategies presented in the previous pages. (Example 1.7 is from the National Institute of Health at http://digestive.niddk.nih.gov/ddiseases/pubs/diverticulosis/index.htm.)

Figure 1.4

Definition of an Annelid

Audience: second-year biology student

Simple Definition Classification **Division 1**	An annelid is a bilaterally symmetric worm whose body is made of specialized segments. The word "annelid" is derived from the Latin anulus, meaning ring. The annelids are members of the phylum and has three classes: (1) polychaeta, (2) oligochaeta, and (3) hirudinae.
Description of Division 1	The polychaetes are exclusively marine annelida. They either swim and crawl freely or live in tubes which they build in the sand. The polychaeta's distinctive head bears eyes and antennae. Excluding the head, the body segments are all alike. Each segment has a pair of lateral appendages, called parapodia, used for respiration and locomotion. On each parapodium are thick bristles called setae. The word "polychaite" comes from the Greek polys, meaning "many".
Etymology Illustration Description	These numerous bristles are characteristic of all polychaetes. For example, the fanworm, a tube dweller, has an iridescent array of pink, green and red setae that wave in the water at the tube entrance.
Description of **Division 2** Etymology Comparison	The class oligichaete, composed of freshwater and terrestrial annelida, includes the earthworm. The word "olichaeta" comes from the Greek oligo, meaning "few", and chaite, meaning "bristles". This reduced number of setae is not the only difference between oligochaetes and parapodia. However, like the polychaetes, the oligichaetes are segmented internally as well as externally.
Description of **Division 3** Etymology Comparison Contrast Description Analogy Illustration	The class hirudinea is comprised solely of leeches, the most specialized of the annelids. The word "hirudinea", derived from the Latin hirudo and hirudini, mean "leech". The leech has the same external segmentations found in polychaetes and oligochaetes. Unlike its two cousins, the leech has no internal segmentation. The leech's body is flattened, lacking parapodia and setae. At each end of the body, the segments are modified, forming suckers. With these suckers, the leech can move its body similar to the locomotion of an inch worm. For example, the bloodsucker, a more familiar leech, uses the suckers to attach itself to a host. The leech is also equipped with a chemical, hirudin, which prevents the coagulation of blood. Since the blood does not coagulate, the leech can feed for extremely long periods.

Example 1.7: Definition of Diverticulosis

The following definition, used in an NIH health-care brochure, shows, from another perspective, how definition devices relate to clear style. Note how definition, visual display, carefully structured sentences, and listing enhances the accessibility of the information.

Diverticulosis and Diverticulitis

Many people have small pouches in their colons that bulge outward through weak spots, like an inner tube that pokes through weak places in a tire. Each pouch is called a diverticulum. Pouches (plural) are called diverticula. The condition of having diverticula is called diverticulosis. About 10% of Americans over the age of 40 have diverticulosis. The condition becomes more common as people age. About half of all people over the age of 60 have diverticulosis.

When the pouches become infected or inflamed, the condition is called diverticulitis. This happens in 10% to 25% of people with diverticulosis. Diverticulosis and diverticulitis are also called diverticular disease.

Figure 1.5

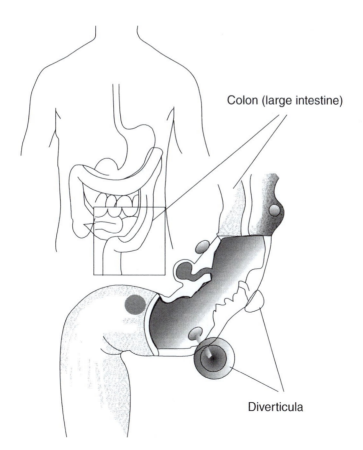

Colon (large intestine)

Diverticula

What Causes Diverticular Disease?

Although not proven, the dominant theory suggests that a low-fiber diet is the main cause of diverticular disease. The disease was first noticed in the United States in the early 1900s. At about the same time, processed foods were introduced into the American diet. Many processed foods contain refined, low-fiber flour. Unlike whole-wheat flour, refined flour has no wheat bran.

Diverticular disease is common in developed or industrialized countries—particularly the United States, England, and Australia—where low-fiber diets are common. The disease is rare in countries of Asia and Africa, where people eat high-fiber vegetable diets.

Fiber is the part of fruits, vegetables, and grains that the body cannot digest. Some fiber dissolves easily in water (soluble fiber). It takes on a soft, jelly-like texture in the intestines. Some fiber passes almost unchanged through the intestines (insoluble fiber). Both kinds of fiber help make stools soft and easy to pass. Fiber also prevents constipation.

Constipation makes the muscles strain to move stool that is too hard. It is the main cause of increased pressure in the colon. This excess pressure might cause the weak spots in the colon to bulge out and become diverticula.

Diverticulitis occurs when diverticula become infected or inflamed. Doctors are not certain what causes the infection. It may begin when stool or bacteria are caught in the diverticula. An attack of diverticulitis can develop suddenly and without warning.

What Are the Symptoms?

Diverticulosis

Most people with diverticulosis do not have any discomfort or symptoms. However, symptoms may include mild cramps, bloating, and constipation. Other diseases such as irritable bowel syndrome (IBS) and stomach ulcers cause similar problems, so these symptoms do not always mean a person has diverticulosis. You should visit your doctor if you have these troubling symptoms.

Diverticulitis

The most common symptom of diverticulitis is abdominal pain. The most common sign is tenderness around the left side of the lower abdomen. If infection is the cause, fever, nausea, vomiting, chills, cramping, and constipation may occur as well. The severity of symptoms depends on the extent of the infection and complications.

What is the Treatment for Diverticular Disease?

A high-fiber diet and, occasionally, mild pain medications will help relieve symptoms in most cases. Sometimes an attack of diverticulitis is serious enough to require a hospital stay and possibly surgery.

Diverticulosis

Increasing the amount of fiber in the diet may reduce symptoms of diverticulosis and prevent complications such as diverticulitis. Fiber keeps stool soft and lowers pressure inside the colon so that bowel contents can move through easily. The American Dietetic Association recommends 20 to 35 grams of fiber each day. The table below shows the amount of fiber in some foods that you can easily add to your diet.

Amount of Fiber in Some Foods

Fruits

Apple, raw, with skin	1 medium	=	4 grams
Peach, raw	1 medium	=	2 grams
Pear, raw	1 medium	=	4 grams
Tangerine, raw	1 medium	=	2 grams

Vegetables

Asparagus, fresh, cooked	4 spears	=	1 gram
Broccoli, fresh, cooked	1/2 cup	=	2.5 grams
Brussels sprouts, fresh, cooked	1/2 cup	=	2 grams
Cabbage, fresh, cooked	1/2 cup	=	1.5 grams
Carrot, fresh, cooked	1/2 cup	=	2.5 grams
Cauliflower, fresh, cooked	1/2 cup	=	1.5 grams
Romaine lettuce	1 cup	=	1 gram
Spinach, fresh, cooked	1/2 cup	=	2 grams
Summer squash, cooked	1 cup	=	3 grams
Tomato, raw	1	=	1 gram
Winter squash, cooked	1 cup	=	6 grams

Starchy Vegetables

Baked beans, canned, plain	1/2 cup	=	6.5 grams
Kidney beans, fresh, cooked	1/2 cup	=	8 grams
Lima beans, fresh, cooked	1/2 cup	=	6.5 grams
Potato, fresh, cooked	1	=	3 grams

Grains

Bread, whole-wheat	1 slice	=	2 grams
Brown rice, cooked	1 cup	=	2.5 grams
Cereal, bran flake	3/4 cup	=	5 grams
Oatmeal, plain, cooked	3/4 cup	=	3 grams
White rice, cooked	1 cup	=	1 gram

The doctor may also recommend taking a fiber product such as Citrucel or Metamucil once a day. These products are mixed with water and provide about 2 to 3.5 grams of fiber per tablespoon, mixed with 8 ounces of water.

Until recently, many doctors suggested avoiding foods with small seeds such as tomatoes or strawberries because they believed that particles could lodge in the diverticula and cause inflammation. However, it is now generally accepted that only foods that may irritate or get caught in the diverticula cause problems. Foods such as nuts, popcorn hulls, and sunflower, pumpkin, caraway, and sesame seeds should be avoided. The seeds in tomatoes, zucchini, cucumbers, strawberries, and raspberries, as well as poppy seeds, are generally considered harmless. People differ in the amounts and types of foods they can eat. Decisions about diet should be made based on what works best for each person. Keeping a food diary may help identify individual items in one's diet.

If cramps, bloating, and constipation are problems, the doctor may prescribe a short course of pain medication. However, many medications affect emptying of the colon, an undesirable side effect for people with diverticulosis.

Diverticulitis

Treatment for diverticulitis focuses on clearing up the infection and inflammation, resting the colon, and preventing or minimizing complications. An attack of diverticulitis without complications may respond to antibiotics within a few days if treated early.

To help the colon rest, the doctor may recommend bed rest and a liquid diet, along with a pain reliever.

An acute attack with severe pain or severe infection may require a hospital stay. Most acute cases of diverticulitis are treated with antibiotics and a liquid diet. The antibiotics are given by injection into a vein. In some cases, however, surgery may be necessary.

Points to Remember

- Diverticulosis occurs when small pouches, called diverticula, bulge outward through weak spots in the colon (large intestine).
- The pouches form when pressure inside the colon builds, usually because of constipation.
- Most people with diverticulosis never have any discomfort or symptoms.
- The most likely cause of diverticulosis is a low-fiber diet because it increases constipation and pressure inside the colon.
- For most people with diverticulosis, eating a high-fiber diet is the only treatment needed.

- You can increase your fiber intake by eating these foods: whole grain breads and cereals; fruit like apples and peaches; vegetables like broccoli, cabbage, spinach, carrots, asparagus, and squash; and starchy vegetables like kidney beans and lima beans.
- Diverticulitis occurs when the pouches become infected or inflamed and cause pain and tenderness around the left side of the lower abdomen.

Questions

One easy way for your students to organize a report is to first determine the purpose and then begin a list of questions that they think the reader will want answered. Then, plan the report around the questions: Draft a title in question format. Begin with an introduction, and then develop the body of the report to answer the questions. Examine Example 1.8, which presents the title as a question: "How Serious Is Antibiotic-Resistant Tuberculosis in India?" The writer answers the main question by presenting supporting information as headings also stated as questions. A student prepared this memo report for a mission trip to India when she discovered that India had a problem with antibiotic-resistant tuberculosis.

Example 1.8: Questions About Tuberculosis

TO: **Jeremy Gray**   **DATE: xxxxxx**
FROM: **Remi Razool**
SUBJECT: **Tuberculosis in India: A General Analysis**

How Serious Is Antibiotic-Resistant Tuberculosis in India?
Many travelers fear a trip to India after reading the story about Mrs. Sheikh and her battle with antibiotic-resistant tuberculosis, also called extensively drug-resistant tuberculosis (XDR T-B) [2],[5]. India has approximately 25% of all the antibiotic-resistant tuberculosis cases in the world, and these are only the reported cases. Tuberculosis can be treated, but recently strains of resistant tuberculosis have developed, and many people with this variety of TB undergo treatment but remain ill [2]. In this analysis, we begin with the facts about general TB, then attempt to answer questions relevant to the problem of drug-resistant tuberculosis.

What Do We Know About General Tuberculosis?

- The bacteria Mycobacterium tuberculosis causes Tuberculosis [5].
- Even though it can be cured, tuberculosis kills 5,000 people each day [1].

- ◆ Vaccine available to humans for the untreatable tuberculosis is still being created and tested.
- ◆ The rate of incidence of people infected with TB is increasing by 1% each year [1].
- ◆ TB spreads through the air when an infected person coughs, sneezes, spits, etc. [5].
- ◆ Someone with a developed immune system is less likely to be infected with TB (i.e. someone who is administered more often in developing countries where JTB is more prevalent) [5].
- ◆ A vaccine for TB called Bacille Calmette Guerin (BCG) is administered more often in developing countries where TB is more prevalent [5].
- ◆ Initial signs and symptoms are weakness, fever, chills, and night sweats.
- ◆ As the disease progresses, more severe symptoms rage the body, such as shortness of breath, chest pain, and coughing blood.

What's the Difference Between TB, MDR-TB, and XDR-TB?

All these forms are a disease that results from the tuberculosis bacteria with different levels of resistance. The MDR-TB resists the two main drugs administered for the treatment of TB. The XCR-TB resists three or more drugs designed for treatment. Poor treatment of general TB is the understood cause of these resistant forms. Early diagnosis and treatment of any form of TB results in the best outcome [5].

Can It Be Treated?

First-line and second-line treatments represent the two categories of medicines available for treatment. First-line treatments provide the more powerful and less harmful drugs, showing the best results in treating patients. These are the first treatments administered. If the first-line treatments do not work, the patient receives second-line treatment, which is not as effective and usually causes more pain. [3]. Mrs. Sheikh underwent first- and second-line drugs, as well as experimental drugs. Although she tested negative for tuberculosis, the side effects of treatment were nearly as ravaging as tuberculosis. Additionally, the treatment was not permanent because the tuberculosis came back [2].

How Likely Are We to Contract MDR-TB or XDR-TBA?

Tuberculosis bacteria spread through the air usually manifests in the lungs. Some people contract it easily, and others remain unaffected, even when in close proximity to someone with the disease, such as Mrs. Sheikh's family [2].

Can We Be Vaccinated for the MDR-TB or XDR-TVB?
A vaccine available to humans for the "untreatable tuberculosis" is still being created and tested in animals [4]. Thus the vaccines now available will not provide adequate protection if a person is exposed to these particular strains of tuberculosis. Before travelling to India, we need to deal with these questions.

References
1. 10 facts about tuberculosis. (n.d.). Retrieved from www.who.int/features/fafiles/tuberculosos/01_en.html
2. Anand, Geeta. "A Woman's Drug-Resistant TB Echoes Around the World." *The Wall Street Journal*, n.p., 8 Sept. 2012. Web. 14 Sept. 2012. <A Woman's Drug-Resistant TB Echoes Around the World>.
3. Bouchane, Killeen. "Virtually Untreatable Tuberculosis." *The Huffington Post*, n.p., 31 Aug. 2012. Web. 14 Sept. 2012. Retrieved from www.huffingtonpost.com/kolleen-bouchane/drug-resistant-tb_b_1845053.html
4. David, N. "Therapeutic Vaccination: Hope for Untreatable Tuberculosis?" *The Journal of Infectious Disease* (2012): Editorial commentary, 13 Aug. 2012. Web.
5. Schiffman, G. (2011, 7 22). *Medicinenet*. Retrieved from www.medicinenet.com/tuberculosis/page2.htm

Supporting Information Headings

Another method to segment your report: State your topic, "The Rise of Drug-Resistant Tuberculosis," and list the supporting information by inserting it beneath headings and subheadings. With word processing, you can move information and rearrange it until you have explained how drug-resistant tuberculosis has developed (Example 1.9). As you draft the report and create the headings, be sure to keep the readers in mind.

In short, list main supporting information as headings and subheadings. Then develop each one. Insert material beneath each heading/subheading.

Example 1.9: Supporting Information Headings About Tuberculosis

TO: **The Rise of Drug-Resistant Tuberculosis**
FROM: **Ridi Razool**
SUBJECT: **Threat of Tuberculosis in India**

Introduction

Tuberculosis (TB), a serious bacterial infection, can be fatal if left untreated. Although numerous antibiotics against tuberculosis are available, the development of drug-resistant forms of TB in several countries over recent decades has made TB a major global health concern. With millions of tons of antibiotics in use worldwide, the selective pressures against rapidly evolving bacteria are sufficient to allow the formation of resistant strains. Not only are resistant strains challenging to treat, but their forms can persist for years, during which horizontal gene transfer of resistant traits to new strains can occur. This report gives a brief overview about TB and examines the recent development of drug-resistant tuberculosis.

The Basics of Tuberculosis

Infection and Symptoms of Tuberculosis

TB is a highly infectious, potentially fatal disease caused by the bacterial strain *Mycobacterium tuberculosis*. [1] It can be primarily confined to the lungs, as in the case of pulmonary TB, or it can affect other areas of the body as well. [1] The main symptom of pulmonary TB is excessive coughing, and patients with more severe symptoms may often cough up blood. [2] Other symptoms include fever, sweats, and chills. [1]

Transmission of Tuberculosis

TB is an airborne disease transmitted when an infected individual coughs, sneezes, or speaks. The resulting infectious droplets can remain suspended in the air for a long time. It is important to note that only individuals with active TB or who are afflicted with the symptoms discussed above, are capable of transmitting the disease in this manner. In contrast, those with latent TB are infected with an inactive form of the bacterium, show no signs or symptoms, and are incapable of spreading the disease to others. [1]

Risk Factors Associated with Tuberculosis

First, people with prolonged exposure to infected individuals have a greater risk of developing TB themselves. This is especially a concern for people who are traveling to countries with high incidence rates of the disease for an extended period of time. India, Mexico, China, and several African countries have a high TB infection rate. [3] However, taking the proper precautions can decrease the likelihood of contracting TB. [1]

Second, people with pre-existing conditions that compromise the immune system have a greater risk of developing active TB. Contrary to popular belief, most people with TB have the latent form of the disease. However, people with HIV, diabetes, and other diseases that weaken the immune system are unable to mount a proper defense against the infection. This weakened condition allows the once-dormant bacteria to become active and proliferate, resulting in the symptoms associated with tuberculosis in the infected patient. [3]

Types of Drug-Resistant Tuberculosis

TB has remained a problem for public health officials because of the recent increase in three different drug-resistant forms of the disease in poor or developing nations. [3]

- ◆ **Multi-drug resistant TB (MDR-TB)** is resistant to the two most commonly prescribed and potent anti-TB drugs, isoniazid and rifampicin. [3]
- ◆ **Extensively drug-resistant TB (XDR-TB)** emerged in the 1990s and is resistant to isoniazid and rifampicin as well as many of the second-line drugs designed to treat infection. [3],[4]
- ◆ **Totally drug-resistant TB (TDR-TB)** is the most dangerous form of tuberculosis since it is resistant to all antibiotics currently available to treat infection. [4] Three cases of TDR-TB have been documented so far, the most recent emerging in India. This apparently incurable form of TB has researchers scouring for a solution.

Causes of Drug-Resistant Tuberculosis

Inadequate Management

Unfortunately, many endemic countries lack the necessary resources to effectively manage drug-resistant TB. Patients in poverty-stricken countries often quit their treatment early due to high costs. [2] On average, drug-resistant tuber-culosis is 200 times more expensive to treat than typical TB. [5] Nevertheless, as with any bacterial infection, it is essential to complete the entire dose to avoid the selection and growth of drug resistant strains. In addition, physicians often mistakenly prescribe the wrong drugs to their patients. Ideally, a patient with tuberculosis should be tested for drug-resistance before subjected to a particular treatment plan. [2],[5] However, according to the WHO, less than 5% of patients diagnosed with the diseases are actually tested. [3] Prescribing the wrong com-bination of antibiotics or wrong dose can increase the likelihood of developing drug-resistant TB. [1]

Lack of New Antibiotics

The development of new antibiotics that can effectively target TB is key to reversing the TB crisis. [4] However, the last antibiotic designed to target TB was released in the 1960s. [2] Because of their high mutation rate, bacteria can easily become resistant to a number of antibiotics and pass on this ability to successive generations. This resistance probably explains why researchers must continu-ously look for new ways to inhibit bacterial function and growth. In addition, current vaccines for tuberculosis lack effectiveness against the drug-resistant forms. [4]

Future Initiatives

The World Health Organization (WHO) has actively advocated the use of drug-resistance TB tests. WHO plans on increasing screening measures and has been actively working to address the co-infection of TB and HIV. [3]

In addition, TB Alliance currently works separately with Bayer and Tibotec to test two new potential drug candidates against drug-resistant TB. [4] Meanwhile, the non-profit organization Aeras is working on developing a new vaccine. [4]

Sources

1. "Tuberculosis (TB)." Centers for Disease Control and Prevention, 13 Sept. 2012. Web. 17 Sept. 2012. <www.cdc.gov/tb/>.
2. Anand, Geeta. "A Woman's Drug-Resistant TB Echoes Around the World." Wall Street Journal, 8 Sept. 2012. Web. 17 Sept. 2012. <http://online.wsj.com/article/SB10000872396390444273704577633431646496346.html>.
3. Global Tuberculosis Control (2011): 1–10. World Health Organization. Web. 17 Sept. 2012. <www.who.int/tb/publications/global_report/en/index.html>.

4. Rowland, Katherine. "Totally Drug-Resistant TB Emerges in India." Nature Publishing Group, 3 Sept. 2012. Web. 17 Sept. 2012. <www.nature.com/news/totally-drug-resistant-tb-emerges-in-india-1.9797>.

5. McNeil, Donald G. "Tuberculosis: Stubborn and Expensive to Treat, Drug-Resistant Strains Show Growth." *New York Times*, 3 Sept. 2012. Web. 17 Sept. 2012. <www.nytimes.com/2012/09/04/science/drug-resistant-tuberculosis-strains-show-growth-worldwide.html>.

Example 1.10: News Article About Tuberculosis
From the Newsdesk, *The Lancet* (Burki, Talha. *The Lancet Infectious Diseases*, Volume 16, Issue 12, 1337–1338).

Multidrug Resistant Tuberculosis: A Continuing Crisis
The multidrug resistant tuberculosis epidemic is a crisis. Despite promising new treatments, gaps in funding and political attention are hampering efforts to stem the disease. Talha Burki reports.

On Oct 13, WHO released its 2016 *Global Tuberculosis Report*. It estimated that last year saw 10.4 million new cases of tuberculosis; improved surveillance from India accounted for most of the 800,000 additional cases compared with 2014. 1.8 million people worldwide (including 400,000 people with HIV) are thought to have died from tuberculosis in 2015, and 60% of the disease burden was concentrated in six countries (India, Indonesia, China, Nigeria, Pakistan, and South Africa). WHO urged their member states to sharply scale-up control efforts, particularly in terms of investment.

The report noted that the available funding for low-income and middle-income countries to tackle tuberculosis in 2016 is roughly US$2 billion short of the amount recommended by the Global Plan. A report by Treatment Action Group (*TAG*), released on Oct 25, expanded on this theme, laying bare the extent of the funding crisis in tuberculosis research and development. In 2015, funding in the field stood at around US$621 million, the lowest level since 2008 and a fall of more than $53 million since the previous year; the biggest decline since TAG started monitoring such matters in 2005. The report's authors point out that the 2011–2015 Global Plan had set funding targets for several areas of research and development, none of which were met. The $1.2 billion invested in drug discovery and development over the 5-year period was less than a third of the $3.7 billion envisaged by the Global Plan.

The two reports put together a mixed picture for multidrug resistant (MDR) tuberculosis. WHO continues to describe the epidemic as a crisis, as it has done for the past 3 years. New cases in 2015 held steady at an estimated 480,000. A further 100,000 people are thought to have rifampicin-resistant disease, but not MDR tuberculosis; in May, 2016, WHO recommended that these patients also be treated with second-line drugs. India, China, and Russia accounted for 45% of the combined burden. "Most high-burden countries have already been surveyed and the data on MDR tuberculosis are quite solid", WHO's Mario Raviglione told *The Lancet Infectious Diseases*. "We know where the problem is huge and where it is not."

In 2012, 18% of patients diagnosed with MDR tuberculosis did not immediately start treatment—a situation Raviglione described as unethical. Last year, only 5% of the 132,000 diagnosed patients were awaiting treatment. But that still means that around 80% of people who are in need of second-line drugs for tuberculosis are going untreated. Moreover, the cure rate for MDR tuberculosis is little more than half. "All we can offer people is awful treatment, with a lot of side-effects that are quite hard to handle, and the need to support them through a 2 year course", said Grania Brigden of the International Union Against Tuberculosis and Lung Disease.

Nonetheless, there are some distinctly hopeful signs. "We have reached a critical mass of new drugs", said Mel Spigelman of the TB Alliance (New York, NY, USA). The advent of bedaquiline and delaminid, the first novel tuberculosis drugs to be approved in more than 40 years, in addition to other compounds in clinical development, has opened up possibilities for new MDR tuberculosis regimens. Despite the underfunding, five such regimens have been put into phase 3 trials since 2011, including the 9-month regimen conditionally recommended by WHO early in 2016. The shortened course showed treatment success rates in excess of 80% during clinical trials.

Two ongoing trials, both of which are being conducted by the TB Alliance, have yielded some promising results. Initial data from the Nix-TB trial testing a combination of bedaquiline, pretomanid, and linezolid for extensively drug-resistant (XDR) tuberculosis found that the majority of patients had negative sputum culture at 2 months; the remaining treated patients had all converted sputum by 4 months. Although linezolid is associated with considerable toxicity, the combination is injection-free and thus far seems safe. The cure rate for XDR tuberculosis, which makes up 10% of MDR cases, stood at 28% last year. The NC005 trial tested a regimen of bedaquiline, pretomanid, and pyrazinamide against drug-sensitive tuberculosis, and the same regimen with the addition of moxifloxacin against MDR tuberculosis. Virtually all of the patients with MDR tuberculosis in the phase 2b trial treated with the quadruple drug regimen showed sputum free of tuberculosis bacteria at 2 months.

"Sometime in the next 3–5 years, we should be able to put together a course of treatment for MDR tuberculosis, consisting of oral pills taken once a day for 4–6 months, that is well tolerated, effective, and affordable", affirmed Spigelman. He believes this could push the cure rate to roughly the same as that for drug-sensitive disease (83% according to the WHO report). And if countries are assured that they can provide good treatment, they might be more inclined to scale-up programmes and track down and diagnose the 400,000 or so hidden cases of MDR disease.

Indeed, there have been significant advances in diagnostics over the past few years. Rapid molecular testing can detect resistance at the same time as identifying tuberculosis. The line probe assay recommended by WHO earlier this year tests for resistance to second-line drugs, and hence suitability for the shortened MDR tuberculosis regimen. There is still no point-of-care test, however, and with the notable exception of South Africa, countries have tended to be slow in rolling out the new tools (some places even seem to prefer microscopy). "We have to ensure that we have proper rapid molecular diagnosis everywhere, at the lowest possible level", stressed Raviglione. "It is just a matter of political will."

The 9-month course for MDR tuberculosis costs around $1000 per patient; other regimens cost $2000–5000. Spigelman expects that the prospective new regimen will drive costs down further but exactly how far is difficult to say. Matters may be complicated by the end of the donation agreement for bedaquiline in 2019. However, a market of 132,000 is not large enough to attract multiple manufacturers. Improving detection rates would help, but probably not enough to generate the volume of sales that could cause the price to dip below $100 per dose. For this to happen, a pan-tuberculosis course is necessary.

If the same regimen could be used on drug-sensitive tuberculosis as on MDR tuberculosis, the benefits would be enormous. The market size would be many times larger, for a start, and cover 99% of patients with tuberculosis. Ideally the course would last for around 1 month, so that patients no longer had to take drugs after their symptoms had disappeared. "That kind of regimen would really simplify the programmatic treatment of tuberculosis—it would be a pivotal moment in turning the tide of the epidemic", explains Brigden. But it is a long way from realisation.

There are currently just two candidates in phase 1 trials. "For MDR tuberculosis, we can certainly make some gains in duration of treatment and side-effects, but we are not going to get the ultimate goal of a 1 month or less regimen that works on drug-sensitive and drug-resistant disease", concluded Brigden. She leads the 3P project, a collaborative effort that aims to jump start the production of a pan-tuberculosis regimen by delinking the end price from research and development costs. "Where antimicrobial resistance might be in 25 years, is where we already are with tuberculosis", Brigden stated. "A curable disease, for which we are running out of treatment options, and not attracting anywhere near enough investment—we have to look at new incentives and ways of funding."

Spigelman is optimistic that the next 5–10 years will see greater advances in MDR tuberculosis than the previous 5–10 years. But he concedes that much depends on resources. "As we make more progress, and get towards more success, the amount of money needed to push things over the finishing line is even greater", Spigelman told *The Lancet Infectious Diseases*. "Phase 3 studies and implementation of new regimens are much more expensive than the discovery of new treatments." Nation states and donors will have to be far more generous than they are at present if progress is to be maintained and consolidated. "The clinical trials that need to be done can stretch out over 10 years or they can be done over 3 or 4 years—it all depends on resources", concluded Spigelman.

A cornerstone of the post-2015 tuberculosis strategy is the target to have no families face catastrophic expenditure because of the disease. This implies some kind of universal health coverage and social protection. No small task, and one that will require strong engagement from government departments outside of the ministry of health. But tuberculosis is one of the world's leading infectious killers; if mitigating its ravages is not the responsibility of government, one would have to wonder what is.

Assignment: Which of the three reports on tuberculosis is easier and quicker to read? Why? What changes could you make to the reports to make them more appealing and easier to read? Partition your class into groups of 3–4 students. Have students discuss the good and bad features of each of the three reports. Have each group revise one of the reports and explain how they improved it.

2

Achieving a Readable Style: Learn Techniques for Clear, Concise, Active Writing

To help your students in *Writing Science Right* you may want to review a few basics of good writing with them. A **sentence** is a group of words that expresses a complete thought. **Style** refers to the overall way to express ideas in a sentence and even the words chosen in a paragraph and in a paper such as a report.

The Paragraph

A reminder: We define a **paragraph** as a group of sentences that begins with a central or topic statement of the paragraph content. The supporting sentences build on the idea stated in the topic sentence and should occur in a logical order. In short:

- ◆ Begin each paragraph with a topic sentence that summarizes content to come.
- ◆ Include only information relevant to the topic sentence.
- ◆ Place sentences in a logical order.
- ◆ Avoid long paragraphs. (No one likes to read long paragraphs!)

Examples for Study

Effective report segments result from effective paragraphs. Examine the following introduction to a science report (Example 2.1). Topic sentences appear underlined. How does a topic sentence contribute to a readable paragraph?

Example 2.1: Introduction to a Science Report

We live on a rotating planet. Every day, as the Earth turns on its axis, we experience the natural cycle of day and night. By day, most humans are busy. During the dark hours of night, we rest. Why do we follow this pattern? Why do we wake up in the morning, often without an alarm clock?

All living things have internal systems that function like clocks. These timekeepers are called biological clocks. In humans these "biological clocks" keep us in sync with our environment. They not only wake us up, they tell us when to sleep. We follow a daily rhythm. But some marine animals follow a different rhythm. Their activities correspond to the rise and fall of ocean tides. The fiddler crab exemplifies one of the sea animals that follows the rhythm of the ocean. A fiddler crab dashes about the beach, finding food and fighting other crabs. The time is low tide, and the crab has a limited amount of time to do its business. Once water begins to rise, the crab returns to its burrow.

The fiddler crab's activities do not coincide with day and night but link to the tides. At low tide, the crab is active. When high tide comes again six hours later, the crab rests. The pattern repeats itself both day and night. In an ocean environment, tides are like a clock. They provide a steady beat that some animals use to regulate their behavior and follow a tidal rhythm.

Male Fiddler Crab

This report about the life rhythm of the male fiddler crab has been prepared to discuss the biological clock of the crabs. The photo, introduction, and two paragraphs set the stage for the report itself. Beginning each paragraph with a topic sentence allows your readers to follow the ideas you are presenting.

All reports begin with an introduction to prepare the reader for the information that follows. Example 2.2 uses a list to draw the reader's eyes to the central idea presented in the paragraph. The topic sentence introduces the paragraph and the list.

Example 2.2: Effective Introduction to a Scientific Report

The Power of Wind Power

Rising energy prices and concern over greenhouse gas have focused congressional attention on energy alternatives, including wind power. Although wind power currently provides only a small fraction of U.S. energy needs, it is growing more rapidly than any other electricity source. Wind energy already plays a major role in several European nations. Countries like China and India are rapidly expanding their capacity to manufacture wind turbines and to integrate wind power into their electricity grids. This report describes high volume, utility-scale wind power issues in the United States. The report is divided into the following sections:

- ◆ Background on wind energy;
- ◆ Wind resources and technology;
- ◆ Industry composition and trends;
- ◆ Wind power economics; and
- ◆ Policy issues.

Using a list emphasizes five items that take front and center in the report.

In this situation, listing highlights the importance of the problem that will be the focus of the report. A traditional paragraph that embedded the list as part of the paragraph would make the concerns harder to notice—see Example 2.3.

Example 2.3: Traditional Paragraph With List

Rising energy prices and concern over greenhouse gas have focused congressional attention on energy alternatives, including wind power.

Although wind power currently provides only a small fraction of U.S. energy needs, it is growing more rapidly than any other electricity source. Wind energy already plays a major role in several European nations. Countries like China and India are rapidly expanding their capacity to manufacture wind turbines and to integrate wind power into their electricity grids. This report describes utility-scale wind power issues in the United States. The report is divided into the following sections: background on wind energy, wind resources and technology, industry composition and trends, wind power economics, and policy issues.

Concise paragraphs that begin with good topic sentences, followed by well-structured sentences of moderate length, create clear, readable papers. In addition, the title and any headings affect the readability of the paragraph by preparing readers for the information to come.

Basic Principles of Effective Style

Effective writers adjust their style to the needs of their readers. Good writers take into consideration (1) their readers' knowledge of the subject and (2) their readers' ability to follow the sentences, considering the context in which they will read the text.

Determine Your Readers' Knowledge of the Subject

The reader's familiarity with the subject will determine how many specialized terms the writer can use. If the reader has a thorough knowledge of the subject, writers can use acronyms, such as DNA, and specialized terms that readers in a specific discipline regularly read and use. If the reader has limited knowledge of the subject, limit the use of specialized vocabulary or define the terms that will be used. Another possibility is to substitute common phrases or words that clearly express the meaning.

Example 2.4 comes from a high school 4-H study packet that describes a ruminant stomach. Notice how the writer defines terms in parentheses.

Example 2.4: From a High School Study Packet
The true (glandular) stomach in the ruminant is preceded by three divisions, or diverticula (lined with stratified squamous epithelium), where food is soaked and subjected to digestion by microorganisms before passing to the digestive tract.

The rumen, reticulum, and omasum of ruminants are collectively known as the fore-stomach. The cardia is located craniodorsally in the dome-shaped atrium ventriculi, which is common to both the rumen and the reticulum. The sulcus ruminoreticularis (esophageal groove), which extended from the cardia to the omasum, is formed by two heavy muscular folds or lips, which can close to direct material from the esophagus into the omasum directly, or open and permit the material to enter the rumen and reticulum.

However, in explaining to 4-H students how the ruminant stomach works, an agricultural extension agent uses a different approach. Note that he uses examples and analogies that will have meaning for middle school students. He includes the technical terms for each part of the ruminant stomach, but he immediately links each term to descriptive terms that would be familiar to his student readers.

Example 2.5: From an Agricultural Extension Agent

The ruminant animals—such as sheep, goats, cattle, deer, antelope, elk, and camels—have a unique stomach system. The word ruminant comes from the Latin word "ruminate," which means to chew over again and implies that ruminants are "cud-chewing" animals. Because of this need to chew their food over and over, their system differs from that of the human or monogastric. Where the human stomach is one large tank, the ruminant's consists of four fermentation and storage tanks connected in series by an intricate network of flexible plumbing. The first three tanks make up the fore-stomach. The fourth tank is comparable to the human stomach and can be called the true stomach.

The rumen is the *first tank*, or stomach, and is quite large. It is responsible for about 75% of the digestive process. When it is full, the rumen holds up to 55 gallons of food, bacteria, and fluids. The main job of the rumen is to store food and keep it until the animal must chew it again. The rumen can be compared to the common blender. When food enters, the rumen begins mixing it with bacteria, which causes the food to start breaking down—or digesting.

The reticulum is *the second stomach* and is relatively small compared to the rumen. The reticulum occupies 5% of the total stomach. Like the rumen, its purpose is storage. The reticulum looks like a cheese grater. The common name for the reticulum is the honeycomb because it is lined with a mucous membrane that contains honeycomb-like compartments. When food enters this stomach, it passes through the honeycomb, which then breaks the food down and shreds it into small pieces. Once the rumen and reticulum break down the food stored in the reticulum, the food moves to the omasum.

The omasum is *the third stomach* and completes the fore-stomach. It is small—occupying about 8% of the total stomach—but it is important to the process of digestion. The omasum's purpose is to make sure the food is broken down enough before it enters the true stomach. This stomach rips, shreds, and crushes the food into a liquid form so that it will not clog the pipe that connects the omasum to the abomasums.

The abomasums, which takes up about 7% of the digestive system, is *the fourth stomach* and is comparable to our own stomach. The abomasums digests what the rumen, reticulum, and omasum break down. At the end of the abomasums is the pipe that allows the food to enter the small intestine. This pipe is call the pylorus and is similar to a strainer. Only properly digested food can enter the pipe.

Note: Conciseness does not equal brevity. Writing concisely means including all that is needed without extra words and phrases that contribute little to the main idea. Brevity means scaling down (rather than completeness of thought).

Adjust the Style to the Readers, the Purpose, and the Context or Setting

Most scientific writing should strive for as much conciseness as possible because of the large quantity of information that readers confront. E-mail messages should have concise paragraphs and concise sentences. Even in complex, highly technical reports, readers value conciseness: the longer the report, the less likely that anyone will read all of it.

Keys to Building Effective Sentences

Watch Sentence Length

Papers composed of consistently long sentences can become difficult to read. Sentence length should vary, but consider revising sentences over 15 words. Even legal documents can benefit from shorter sentences and have improved as a result of the plain English laws that now govern insurance policies and many other legal documents in various states. Many government entities want their public documents written in concise, easily understood sentences.

Excessively complex:

Familiar to all are the rhythmic changes in innumerable processes of animals and plants in nature. Examples of phenomena geared to the 24-hour solar day produced by rotation of the earth relative to the sun are sleep movements of plant leaves and petals, spontaneous activity in numerous animals, emergence of flies from their pupal cases, color changes of the skin in crabs, and wakefulness in man.

Sample patterns of daily fluctuations, each interpretable as adaptive for the species are discussed here. Rhythmic phenomena linked to the 24-hour and 50-minute lunar-day period of rotation of the earth relative to the moon are most conspicuous among intertidal organisms whose lives are dominated by the ebb and flow of the ocean tides. Everyone knows that there are individuals who are able to awaken morning after morning at the same time within a few minutes. Are they awakened by sensory cues received unconsciously, or is there some "biological clock" that keeps accurate account of the passage of time? Students of the behavior or animals in relation to their environment have long been interested in the biological question.

More easily understood:

Everyone knows individuals able to awaken morning after morning at the same time within a few minutes. Are they awakened by sensory cues received unconsciously, or is there some "biological clock" that keeps accurate account of the passage of time? Students of that behavior and of animals in relation to their environment have long been interested in the biological question.

Most animals show a rhythmic behavior pattern of one sort or another. For instance, many animals that live along the ocean shores have behavior cycles which repeat with the ebb and flow of the tides, each cycle averaging about 12.5 hours in length.

If you expect readers whom you will have to interest in your topic, to read what you have written, you may need to add some drama to your writing.

More easily understood and compelling:

One of the greatest riddles of the universe is the uncanny ability of living things to carry out their normal activities with clocklike precision at a particular time of the day, month, and year. Why do oysters plucked from a Connecticut bay and shipped to a Midwest laboratory continue to time their lives to ocean tides 800 miles away? How do potatoes in hermetically sealed containers predict atmospheric pressure trends two days in advance? What effects do the lunar and solar rhythms have on the life habits of man? Living things clearly possess powerful adaptive capacities—but the explanation of whatever strange and powerful forces are involved in this behavior continues to challenge science.

In short, understand your topic, determine what sentence length and word choice will best appeal to the reader, and then choose the tone of your message. **Be aware of the characteristics of bad and good writing.**

Characteristics of Bad and Good Writing

Bad Writing	Good Writing
few action verbs per sentence	many verbs per sentence
excessive *is/are* verb forms	specific action verbs
abstract nouns	actual, tangible nouns
many prepositional phrases	few prepositional phrases
passive voice	active voice
key words are separated (by other words)	actor–action and subject–verb connections are clear (usually because they are close together)
long, rambling sentences	specific, precise sentences
one sentence contains many distinct ideas that are not clearly connected to each other	main idea of each sentence is easy to find and follow
sentences must be read several times	sentence meaning is clear after one reading

Keep Subjects and Verbs Close Together

A recipe for sentence clarity: *keep the subject of the sentence and the verb close together and emphasize verbs.* The more verbs in a sentence, the sharper and more direct the sentence. Be aware of the number of verbs in relationship to the number of words in a sentence. The verb-to-word ratio controls the directness of the meaning. Examine the following sentences: The more verbs the clearer the sentence.

> s   v   s   v

John *enjoyed* physics because he *learned* the basics easily. (verb/word ratio 2/9)

versus

> s   v

John's enjoyment of physics *was dependent* on his ease of learning the basics of science. (verb/word ratio 1/14)

In this simple example, you can see the point: the more verbs, the sharper the sentence. (In addition, the sole verb in the second sentence is passive—*was dependent*—instead of active—*enjoyed, learned.*)

Let's take this method a step further: Lengthy sentences become less distracting to the reader if the writer structures them to improve clarity and readability. To achieve clarity, build sentences with clauses and as many verbs and verbals (to + a verb) as possible. For example, this sentence is developed from three clauses:

When they plan science proposals, researchers consider a variety of options because they need research funds. (16 words)

1) *When they* <u>*plan*</u> *science proposals*
2) *researchers* <u>*consider*</u> *a variety of options*
3) *because they* <u>*need*</u> *research funds.*

Note that the sentence follows the three guidelines: interlocking clauses (three in this sentence); specific action verbs (plan, recommend, and need); subject next to the verb in each clause:

1) *they plan*
2) *researchers consider*
3) *they need*

The sentence has a verb/word ratio of 3/17.

Now, let's see what would happen if the writer did not follow the guidelines and avoided verbs:

In their planning for science proposals, a variety of approaches *are considered* by researchers because of their serious need for project funding. (21 words)

The verb/word ratio is 1/21. The sentence lacks directness and conciseness. Compare the two versions. Can you see the difference?

> The more verbs and verbals a writer uses, the easier time the reader has in understanding the sentence(s). The actor, or subject should be followed with an active verb that identifies what the actor does.

For most writing, use specific, concrete subjects and verbs.

Instead of:

There *is* now no effective existing mechanism for introducing into the beginning initiation and development stages requirements on how to guide employees on how *to minimize* errors in product development efforts.

(verb/word ratio 3/31; one "is" verb and two verbals)

Use:

The company *has* no way *to guide* employees on how *to minimize* product development errors during the early development stages.

(verb/word ratio 3/20; note that the sentence begins with the actor in the subject position and includes two verbals)

Note: When a sentence lacks a clear subject/agent doing the action (verb), writers can often drift into the phrases "there is, there are, there was, there were," which have no meaning and deter conciseness and directness.

Direct/indirect words also affect tone:

a. *We encourage you to prepare for large volumes of rain that can be expected in California so take every measure to protect your property.*
b. We expect heavy rainfall in California, so be prepared.

Note that (b) is easier to read than (a). The tone of (a) also sounds pompous.

Write Squeaky-Clean Prose

The following excerpt from *DNA: The Secret of Life*, one of the most important science books of the 20th century, addresses readers interested in science who have a basic understanding of genetics. Note the structure of each sentence, the use of topic sentences, and the development of each paragraph:

The great size of DNA molecules posed a big problem in the early days of molecular biology. To come to grips with a particular gene—a particular stretch of DNA—we would have to devise some way of isolating it from all the rest of the DNA that sprawled around it in either direction. But it was not only a matter of isolating the gene; we also needed some way of "amplifying" it: obtaining a large enough sample of it to work with. In essence we needed a molecular editing system: a pair of molecular scissors that could cut the DNA text into manageable sections; a kind of molecular glue pot that would allow us to manipulate those pieces; and finally a molecular duplicating machine to amplify the pieces that we had cut out and isolated. We wanted to do the equivalent of what a word processor can now achieve: to cut, paste, and copy DNA.

Developing the basic tools to perform these procedures seemed a tall order even after we cracked the genetic code. A number of discoveries made in the late sixties and early seventies, however, serendipitously came together in 1973 to give us so-called "recombinant DNA" technology—the capacity to edit DNA. This was no ordinary advance in lab techniques. Scientists were suddenly able to tailor DNA molecules, creating ones that had never before been seen in nature. We could "play God" with the molecular underpinning of all of life. This was an unsettling idea to many people. Jeremy Rifkin, an alarmist for whom every new genetic technology has about it the whiff of Dr. Frankenstein's monster, had it right when he remarked that recombinant DNA "rivaled the importance of the discovery of fire itself."

Source: Watson, James. *DNA: The Secret of Life*, pp. 87–88. Knopf, 2003. Used by permission.

This excerpt uses a variety of sentences of moderate length, close subject-verb patterns, familiar words, and a description of recombinant DNA in words easily understood by the nonscientific reader: the passage concisely and picturesquely expresses the meaning of recombinant DNA.

Avoid Pompous Language—Write to Express, Not Impress

The concept of simplicity relates to the concept of naturalness. Writers often believe they must sound learned, aloof, and sophisticated to impress readers. The idea that direct writing lacks sophistication frequently derives from writing done in high school where teachers encourage students to expand their vocabularies. Academic writing in college reinforces the importance of using jargon-laden language to convince the professor that the student knows the subject and the terminology or vocabulary of the discipline. Instructors may reward students for writing ponderous verbiage in research papers. However, particularly in the science fields, verbose writing may be ignored or misread by readers who are only interested in gleaning information relevant to their work.

Remember that writing exists for human beings to communicate. Few of us enjoy reading writing that seems harder to read than it needs to be. What constitutes "difficult" writing depends on the reader, the topic, and the purpose of the paper. Direct, concise writing that uses a conversational style will usually be appreciated by most readers. Using shorter rather than longer sentences also helps readers follow your thoughts. Consider:

Please give immediate attention to ensure that the pages of all science reports prepared for distribution are numbered sequentially and in a place of optimum visibility. This is needed to facilitate our ability to refer to items during meetings.

Versus:

Please correctly number the pages of all documents. Place numbers in the upper right-hand corner. Sequential numbering helps us locate material during meetings.

Or:

Please number all pages in order.

Avoid Excessive Use of "Is/Are" Verb Forms

Choosing specific, concrete verbs for clarity means avoiding forms of the "be" verb whenever possible. As the following sentences illustrate, excessive use of "be" verbs often obscures action verbs. Many times, a "be" verb presents the best choice (as this sentence exemplifies). However, writers can lessen the tendency to rely on "be" verbs by doing the following:

1) Avoid beginning sentences with *there is* or *there are, there was* or *there were*.
2) Avoid beginning sentences with phrases such as *it is clear that, it is evident that,* and *it should be noted that.*
3) Choose a specific verb rather than *is, are, was,* and *were* verb forms.

"Be" verbs often create a longer, less direct sentence:

Delegation is a means of lessening the manager's work load.

Versus:

Managers who delegate *reduce* their work load.

"Be" words introduce extra words:

My decision *is based on the assumption* that his statement *is erroneous.*

Versus:

My decision *assumed* his statement *is erroneous.*

As these examples and the ones that follow show, the clearest sentences focus on the agent and the action (the verb):

There are two methods presently available for testing research samples.

Shorter and clearer:

Two available methods can test research samples.

Wordy:

There are several national and global organizations dedicated to pro-moting environmental sustainability for health care facilities.

Shorter and clearer:

Several national and global organizations promote environmental sustainability for health care facilities.

Use Active Voice for Clarity

The structure of a sentence—the arrangement of words—affects the clarity of the sentence. In active voice, the actor that does the action occurs next to the verb. The actor and the action both appear in the sentence, and the actor appears as the subject of the sentence.

Actor   verb

The department teaches Chemistry II every spring term.

Actor   verb

The science coordinator refused to allow freshmen to take Biology II.

The result? Clear, concise, direct sentences.

Before:

(A)   Attempts were made by the science faculty to assess the new course revisions.

After:

actor   verb

(B)   The science faculty attempted to assess the new course revisions.

Sentence (A) uses passive voice. Sentence (B) uses active voice: the actor (staff) occurs as the subject and appears next to the verb (*attempted*).

Research to determine the most readable sentence structures indicates that active voice sentences are more readable than passive sentences. Readers often need the actor placed near the action (the verb) to determine the sentence meaning. The subject and verb contain the essence of the sentence. The following examples illustrate this concept. Imagine a sign:

The Door to the Science Labs Is to Be Locked at 6:00 P.M.

This sentence, which does not specify the actor (the person doing the action), could mean either of the following:

The janitor [or some designated person] will lock the door at 6:00 P.M.
The last person leaving the building at 6:00 P.M. must lock the science
   lab door.

As both revisions illustrate, to understand a sentence, readers need to know the actor and the action carried out by the actor. Sentences should indicate who or what performs the action.

Passive voice sentences often intentionally do not include the actor or agent doing the action to hide responsibility. The result may produce a sentence more verbose and less accurate than an active voice version. Passive voice sentences often use "there is" and "there are" constructions. Even in engineering writing, such as articles for academic journals, many editors want active voice sentences because of the increased clarity of the sentences. As in the examples below, the use of active subjects will usually make an explanation easier to read and easier to understand:

Before:

With the growing request of high quality multimedia service, especially in portable systems, efficient algorithms for audio and/or video data processing have been developed. These algorithms have the characteristics of high complexity data-intensive computation. For these applications, there exist two extreme implementations. One is software implementation running on a general purpose processor and the other is hardware implementation in the form of application-specific integrated circuit (ASIC). In the first case, it is flexible enough to support various applications but may not yield sufficient performance to cope with the complexity of application. In the second case, optimization is better in respect of both power and performance but only for a specific application. A coarse-grained reconfigurable architecture fills the gap between the two approaches, providing higher performance than software implementation and wider applicability than hardware implementation.

Try to write this example more concisely. Breaking long sentences into shorter ones and creating short paragraphs can also produce clarity.

Before:

To ensure quality of manufactured products, a crucial step is to take coordinate measurements of the geometric features to reconstruct product surface and then to check their compliance with tolerance specifications: my research develops a method to integrate the coordinate measurements from measuring devices of different resolutions for a better reconstruction of the product surface.

After:

To ensure quality of manufactured products, researchers must take coordinated measurements of the geometric features. The goal: to reconstruct product surface and then check surface compliance with tolerance specifications.

My research develops a method to integrate the coordinate[d] measurements from measuring devices of different resolutions to better reconstruct the product surface.

Avoid Using Longer Words When Shorter Ones Will Do Just as Well

To write concise sentences, use clear, concise words and phrases.
(Write to express, not to impress.)

Instead of:	Write:	Instead of:	Write:
accumulate	gather	implement	carry out
acquire	get	initiate	begin
acquaint	tell	maximum	most
activate	begin	modification	change
aggregate	total	nevertheless	but, however
assist	help	objective	aim
communicate	write, talk, tell	optimum	best
compensation	pay	personnel	people, staff
consequently	so	procure	get
continue	keep up	purchase	buy
demonstrate	show	terminate	end
discontinue	stop	transmit	send
endeavor	try	utilize	use
facilitate	ease, simplify		

Eliminate Words That Add Nothing to the Meaning of the Sentence

Reread your own sentences to delete any unnecessary words.

to the extent that	in view of
with respect to	in as much as
as a matter of fact	for the purpose
with reference to	in order
in connection with	as already stated

Avoid Words That Sound Knowledgeable Without Being Specific

Many are technical words that have been overused and poorly adapted to nontechnical situations.

parameters	warrants further investigation
broad-based	paradigm
contact	dynamics
impact	infrastructure
input/output	longitudinal study
conceptualize	matrix
meaningful	resource utilization
multifaceted	systematized
methodized	prioritize

Avoid Wordiness

These phrases can be pared down to avoid repetition.

absolutely complete	human volunteer
absolutely essential	green in color
my personal opinion	point in time
necessary essentials	sincere and earnest
basic fundamentals	small in size
complete absence	summarize briefly
consensus of opinion	miniscule
each and every	thought and consideration
exactly identical	true facts
example to illustrate	very unique
few in number	first and foremost
consideration was given	I considered
prior to the	before
at the present writing	now
effect an improvement	improve

(continued overleaf)

Continued	
cognizant of	know
endeavor	try
viable alternative	possibility
in regard/reference to	about
in the normal course of procedure	normally
in this day and age	today
in my opinion	I believe
it is our opinion	we think
on a daily basis	daily
on the grounds that	because
without further delay	now

Style Exercises

Sentence Style

Ask your students to decide which recommendations in this chapter operate in the revisions of the following sentences. Why do these principles result in clearer, more concise revisions?

1. A stroke is an increasingly common problem associated with the brain. It is caused when a vein or artery in the brain is obstructed. This results in loss of consciousness from the loss of oxygen in the brain.

   Revision: A stroke, an obstruction in a vein or artery in the brain, results in loss of consciousness because the brain does not receive oxygen.

2. There is another method that is more invasive to the patient but proves to be successful enough to treat stroke.

   Revision: Another, more invasive, method proves successful in treating stroke.

3. There are many proposed solutions for ridding the U.S. of oil dependency.

   Revision: Many proposed solutions target reduction of U.S. oil dependency.

4. A significant amount of new research has come out recently about a bodily phenomenon called brown fat. Brown fat is regarded with interest because of its potential use as a new therapy for obese patients. Brown fat is nothing new—it's been known for centuries as "baby fat," the stuff that makes newborn infants so adorably chubby.

   Revision: Recent research on human "brown fat" shows that it may help obese patients. Brown fat, known for centuries as "baby fat," makes newborn infants chubby.

5. People in this field work in hospitals and dedicate their time to the mental well-being of children in hospitals as well as to helping the parents be able to support their children and cope with the trauma.

   Revision: People in this field work in hospitals. These professionals focus on the mental well-being of hospitalized children and help the parents support their children as they cope with trauma.

6. Asperger's Syndrome, sometimes called high functioning Autism Disorder, is a disability in young people that is frequently overlooked by educators and medical personnel.

   Revision: Educators and medical personnel frequently overlook Asperger's Syndrome, a high functioning Autism Disorder occurring in young people.

7. Even though Hurricane Gustav left its mark, there was a minimal amount of damage to the town, and finally there was a sigh of relief regarding energy prices.

   Revision: Even though Hurricane Gustav left its mark, the town suffered minimal damage and gave a sigh of relief regarding energy prices.

8. A shoemaking company has signed a deal to share military technology to make their shoes waterproof, at the same time making the fabric breathable.

   Revision: A shoemaking company has signed a deal to share military technology, making their shoes both waterproof and breathable.

9. There are many issues facing New Orleans related directly to hurricanes and tropical storms. Recently most of the problems caused from these storms have been traced back to the loss of wetlands of New Orleans during the past century. Despite recent pushes by community and political leaders in New Orleans to help restore these, very little has been done, leaving much of the city vulnerable to hurricanes and allowing sea level to continue to rise.

   Revision: New Orleans faces many issues related to hurricanes and tropical storms. Most problems caused by these storms have occurred because of loss of wetlands around New Orleans during the past century. The city has become more vulnerable to hurricanes as the sea level continues to rise. Little has been done, despite efforts by community and political leaders, to restore wetlands.

10. Efforts were made on the part of the director's committee for completion of an evaluation of the recommendations of the report.

    Revision: The director's committee tried to complete their evaluation of the report recommendations.

Have your students revise the following excerpts according to principles presented in this chapter.

1. There are several national and global organizations dedicated to promoting environmental sustainability for health care facilities.
2. Though there have been numerous economic anthropology studies in Mexico, they have largely been in three locations.
3. The intervening steps taken in the site are with the intention to make the site more attractive. This is done by establishing services, heading offices, cultural centers, and commercial firms in the downtown district.
4. For adequate housing in such circumstances, this paper here presents a model. The model is a step-by-step development process which is aimed at empowering the users. This process includes:*
   – Innovative financing
   – Creating employment opportunity
   – Make the users aware of sustainable systems for drinking water, sewage disposal, other utilities, and shelter improvement
   – Demonstrate the knowledge of the mentioned systems through a construction of a public facility for them.
   – Transfer the knowledge by employing the users in the construction and maintenance of the facility.

---

*Note: Teaching usage works best when it is included in all exercises rather than by itself. Parallel structure can be a huge problem for many students, and they can often more easily identify it as a problem when they are evaluating a bulleted list like this one.

---

5. At the same time, these fuels must be easy to burn cleanly. This is typically characteristic of liquid and gaseous fuels. Lastly, it is best that the fuel be all liquid or a gas because of the ability to pump both. This means that the existing infrastructure can be used to distribute the fuel.
6. Lots of money around the world is poured into cancer research.
7. There has been success using lymphotropic paramagnetic nanoparticles for imaging prostate cancer.
8. There is plenty of money and room for big companies to get their foot in and discover new technologies to fight cancer.
9. Recently there has been a surge in research and development for a material called grapheme. One area grapheme is being applied to is solar cells.

10. Sustainable development is the process of moving human activities into a pattern that can be perpetually sustained. It is an approach that seeks to meet the needs of the present while protecting the resources that will be needed in the future.

Paragraph and Visual Style

Style also involves using visuals to help readers "see" your meaning. Visual displays of concepts are extremely important, so we introduce the concept here and then develop it further in Chapter 4 on oral presentations.

Examine the examples in Figures 2.1 and 2.2. The example in Figure 2.1 targets students in a middle-school science class. The example in Figure 2.2 targets adults in a continuing education course on birding. How do the drawings of birds flocking affect the readability of each example? Ask students to write two paragraphs describing the style of each example based on the style principles and keys in this chapter. Then have them revise the text and the visuals in Figure 2.1.

Figure 2.1 A definition of flocking for middle school students

What Is Flocking?

Why do hawks fly together in a group? Haven't you noticed that you often see hawks flying together rather than just one hawk flying all by itself?

Soaring birds, such as hawks and vultures, migrate in flocks, groups of birds that fly close together. Scientists have studied why hawks like flying together in flocks. These scientists have concluded that hawks travel as a group to help each other fly in the right direction. Another possible reason is that a group of hawks traveling together can find thermals more easily than can one hawk flying all by itself.

What are thermals and why are they important to soaring birds? Thermals are bubbles of warm air that rise from the ground into the sky. Hawks get inside these thermals and circle high in the air. When they reach the top of the thermal, they glide down to the bottom of the next one, then up again and down until they arrive home. Their flight looks like this:

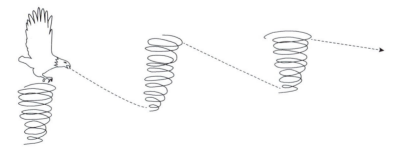

So hawks, by using thermals, which are natural warm air currents, can circle and glide rather than flap their wings. As a result, they save energy as well as time. That's why you see hawks flying together. Working together, they can find these thermals, rather than looking for them alone.

Figure 2.2 A definition of flocking for a more mature audience

The Function of Flocking in Long-Distance Soaring Migrants

Studies by ornithologists have shown that soaring birds migrate in flocks. Since most migratory broad-winged hawks are observed in flocks and form groups even in the early morning, flocking must have some specific advantages for these raptors.

Some researchers believe that flocking assists hawks in navigating and in orienting themselves in the proper direction. Other biologists conclude that flocking enables hawks to locate thermals, the rising currents of warm air that allow the birds to soar and thus gain altitude. A hawk that has reached the top of a thermal can then glide down to the base of the next thermal, soar up, and glide down again, thermal-hopping until it reaches its destination.

Some researchers also suggest that thermal travel conserves energy and time for migrating raptors hawks' ability to find these thermals for soaring (wings spread for circular motion) and gliding (wings spread for forward motion). This method of flight is essential to conserve energy. In contrast, flapping flight uses over five times as much energy. Thermals also increase hawks' flight speed, since they use air currents both while soaring within the thermal and while gliding to the next one, rather than relying on their own powered flight.

These researchers also believe that flocking behavior enhances hawks' chances for encountering these life-saving thermals. A group of hawks moving together, as in (a) will more likely find thermals, which are produced randomly by the heating of the earth's surface, than will a bird traveling alone across the vast expanse of sky, as in (b). Interestingly,a computer simulation program has been designed to find optimum dimensions for encountering thermals produced by a geometric shape similar to that of hawk flocks.

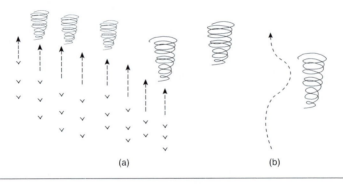

(a)   (b)

3

Reporting Research Findings: Explore the Use of Science Articles and Letters

This chapter introduces you and your students to science articles and provides assignments that allow students to study and practice principles that define good science good writing. We include example articles from *The Lancet*, one of the most prestigious science journals. Assignments ask students to shorten articles to make writing more concise and interesting to non-specialist readers. The articles deal with major science/medical issues—diseases transmissible from animals to humans.

Recognizing that human health, animal health, and ecosystem health are inextricably linked, One Health seeks to promote, improve, and defend the health and well-being of all species by enhancing cooperation and collaboration between physicians, veterinarians, and other scientific health and environmental professionals and by promoting strengths in leadership and management to achieve these goals.

Thus, this chapter illustrates the One Health concept, which combines research in veterinary diseases and health with human medicine and research. One Health has increased as a major issue as people fight for life and safety. The article below shares some of this attitude and information about this concept. The short abstract provides a succinct rationale for this approach to human and animal medicine. Our fondest hope: that you and your students will recognize the value and urgency of these global health issues and come away from this book and this chapter more aware of the health problems the world faces.

Short science reports, often called letter reports, science letters, perspectives, and commentaries, provide a good way for your students to report their research findings. Editorials also offer an outlet for presenting an argument for a science issue. Long science articles are hard to write and even harder to get accepted. Short science reports are much easier to write, particularly when the subject can provide limited coverage but interest readers in learning more. Current issues, such as viruses, diseases, pesticides, and vaccines, provide excellent topics.

All reports require introductions that state the direction the report will take, as discussed in Chapters 1 and 2, in addition to an informative title and statements that explain the importance of the topic, and the major points that will be discussed. The science letter in Example 3.1, targeting the threat to the bee population, exemplifies one topic within the One Health issues. We provide a range of articles from which you can choose. Check this book's Taylor & Francis website to see additional articles we have provided.

Example 3.1:
Why bees? Without bees, humans and animals would have difficulty eating!

Policies to Protect Diminishing Bee Populations in the United States
National High School Journal of Science
Posted By: Johyun Lee August 28, 2016—OA

Honey bees are pollinators that have a strong influence on ecological relationships, ecosystem conservation and genetic variation in plants, with pollination occurring in a variety of ways: wind, animals, self-pollination and sexual reproduction. According to Greenpeace, an estimated 87.5% of flowering plants are pollinated by animals, and can increase fruit or seed in 75% of the world's food crops [1]. Greenpeace also shows that although grains such as wheat, rice and corn rely mainly on wind for pollination, nutrient-rich fruit and vegetable crops, along with some fodder crops, rely on insects. Of all insect pollinators, bees are the leading species [2].

The pollination process is integral to the production of our food supply and economy. According to the U.S. Department of Agriculture, "more than three-fourths of the world's flowering plants rely on pollinators . . . [helping] produce one out of every three bites of food Americans eat" ("Yearly Survey Shows Better Results for Pollinators, but Losses Remain Significant." United States Department of Agriculture Agricultural Research Service). Bees secure global diversity and food security for humans. *A. mellifera*, specifically, pollinates over 130 different species of fruits and vegetables, and is responsible for pollinating approximately 80% of all American agricultural food crops, worth an estimated $40 billion USD per year [3]. Thus, the effect of bees on the economy, as well as on ecosystem diversity, is significant.

Farmers use fungicides and pesticides to increase yield of production. These pesticides, including neonicotinoids, pyrethroids, cyclodienes, organophosphates, carbamates and oxadiazoles, have been shown to have an effect on the "enzyme activity, development, oviposition behavior, offspring sex ratios, mobility, naviga- tion and orientation, feeding behavior, learning and immune function" of bees (Pettis 2013). This exposure to pesticides, along with the effects of invasive para- sites, climate change and habitat loss, contributes to the declining global bee populations that have been occurring since 2006, especially in North America and Europe. Neonicotinoids in particular have received notable attention due to their potential risks to the ecosystem, as "chemicals persist in the environment, thereby promoting their contact with non-target organisms such as pollinating bees" (Wil- liams 2015).

To investigate the actual impacts of the pesticides, scientists gathered pollen from different crops such as almonds, apples, blueberries, cranberries, cucumbers, pumpkins, and watermelons. While analyzing the pesticide concentration in each pollen sample, the scientists put the main focus on the total number of pesticides, dividing the results into 10 different categories: insecticides, fungicides, herbi- cides, carbamates, cyclodienes, formamidines, neonicotinoids, organophosphates, oxadiazines and pyrethroids. Scientists also collected 210 healthy honey bees from Bee Research Laboratory. The bees in the experimental trials were all equally healthy, which effectively made the honey bee's initial health a control variable. Bees were fed pollen for 2–4 days in order to examine the impact of the pesticides (Pettis, J. S., Lichtenberg, E. M., Andree, M., Stitzinger, J., Rose, R., & VanEngelsdorp, D. (2013, July 24)).

Thirty-five different pesticides were detected in the sampled pollen, includ- ing high fungicide loads. The insecticides esfenvalerate and phosmet were at a concentration higher than their median lethal dose in at least one pollen sample. While fungicides are typically seen as fairly safe for honey bees, we found an increased probability of *Nosema* infection in bees that consumed pollen with a higher fungicide load. *Nosema* infections contain intracellular parasites that can multiply in living honey bees, and deteriorate their immune systems. Once the bees are affected, they have difficulty reproducing and nurturing offspring. Infec- tion in autumn can also lead to poor overwintering and performance in spring. Queen bees can also be superseded when affected.

In general, pollens contain excessive fungicides. The research suggests that exposure to heavy fungicide loads can make bees more sensitive, increasing their risk of being infected by the *Nosema* disease. Scientists also found that a few pesticides, such as Esfenvalerate and coumaphos, play a role in Colony Collapse

Figure 3.1

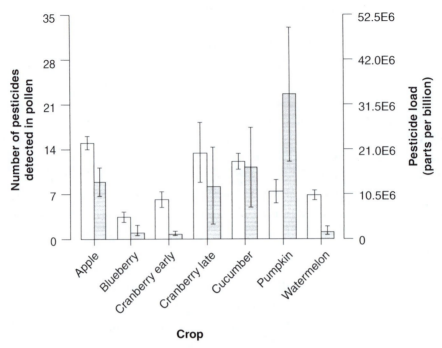

Disorder, one of the main threats to bee colonies. These results suggest that insecticides used to help the growth of plants are actually detrimental to pollinator's health.

What is concerning is not only the fact that 35 pesticides were found from the pollens, but also the fact that the concentration of some pesticides were very high. Esfenvalerate, for example, was "measured at 0.216 ppm in pollen collected by bees in a cucumber field, and phosmet (LD50?=?8.83 ppm) at 14.7 ppm in one apple orchard" [4]. Data of the scientists suggest that some of the bee colonies are being exposed to dangerously high concentration of pesticide loads. Moreover, research suggests that simultaneous exposure to pesticides can have lethal effects on development, reproduction, learning and memory, and foraging behavior.

Apart from *Nosema* infection, insecticides like neonicotinoids have also produced detrimental effects on the queen bee's health, which is crucial to the survival of bee colonies. As noted in a study conducted to show the effect of neonicotinoid exposure to queen bees, "queen failure has been proposed to be a major driver of managed honey bee colony losses, yet few data exist concerning effects of environmental stressors on queens" (Williams 2015). As such, the study focuses on the reproductive success, anatomy and physiology of the queens after being exposed to the pesticides. The hypothesis of this study was that "exposure to field-realistic concentrations of neonicotinoid pesticides would significantly reduce honey bee queen performance due to possible changes in behavior, and reproductive anatomy and physiology" [4]. This hypothesis was tested by exposing "developing honey bee queens to environmentally-relevant concentrations of the common neonicotinoid pesticides thiamethoxam and clothianidin" [4]. Both pesticides are widely applied in global agro-ecosystems and are accessible to pollinators such as social bees, but are currently subjected to two years of restricted use in the European Union because of concerns over their safety. The basic procedure that followed is that queens were allowed to sexually mature, and the production of worker bee offspring was observed for 4 weeks. Data shows that 25% fewer queens were alive than in the controls, with 38% fewer queens in the experimental trials producing worker bees than in the controls [4]. There was also 34% less reproductive success in the queen bees that had been exposed to neonicotinoid doses [4].

The results show the fragility of queen physiology, anatomy and reproductive success. By being exposed to field-realistic doses of neonicotinoids, the development of social queen bees was severely hindered. Even within 4 weeks' time, there were very notable effects. One change in anatomy that occurred was ovariole hyperplasia in the neonicotinoid-exposed queen bees. The larger ovary sizes suggests that neonicotinoid has a direct impact on the reproductive systems of queen bees, although it cannot be determined through this study exactly how this may impact reproductive processes. The decrease in stored spermatozoa and spermatozoa quality can be inferred to be a limiting factor to queen longevity, since queen bees that do not properly or successfully develop anatomically and sexually are often replaced in bee colonies. These findings show that even common pesticides can have significant effects on queen anatomy and physiology. As a result, in order to protect *Apis mellifera*, it is necessary for greater knowledge on lethal and sub lethal pesticide doses, as well as greater evaluation of pesticide safety.

Predictions

Given the available data, if no actions are taken to protect *Apis mellifera* colonies, within twenty years, some U.S. states will no longer have any *Apis mellifera* colonies. Looking at Figure 3.1, some states have already lost more than half of their honey bee colonies. Humans will lose one of the few pollinators on Earth, endangering more than just our food sources. Plants that need the help of honey bees will have difficulty reproducing, which may lead to decreased species diversity in plants. Fewer plants would mean less energy for consumers ranging from insects to humans. There would be less energy in the ecosystem in general, as primary producers number will significantly decrease, which would eventually lead to decrease in energy levels in the food web. The ecosystem would not be able to function as it did before in homeostasis.

Solution

Given the available data, if no actions are taken to protect *Apis mellifera* colonies, within twenty years, some U.S. states will no longer have any *Apis mellifera* colonies, which would have a disastrous impact on global ecosystems. To protect *Apis mellifera*, the U.S. can follow in the steps of the European Union, which has placed a ban on 3 types of neonicotinoids that have proven to have detrimental effects. As summarized in the queen bee study [4], neonicotinoids can have a significant impact on bee development, maturity and behaviour, and can affect the success of bee colonies. As a result of concerns on reduced bee diversity and distribution, the E.U., as of December 1st, 2013, has restricted the use of clothianidin, imidacloprid and thiamethoxam in seed coatings. According to the Pesticide Action Network Europe, they have a table listing pesticides that could be replaced by natural predators or other alternatives.

Additionally, the U.S. could also place greater regulation measures on farmers of key food crops, limiting the amount of pesticide and pesticide categories that can be used within specific periods of time. Another potential solution would be for the U.S. to increase knowledge on the subject and educate the farmers on the effects of pesticide use on the environment and its included species. Since the primary motivation behind pesticide use is to increase farming productivity, farmers should be aware that such practices not only endanger bees, but also risk biomagnification, which increases pesticide load concentration down the food chain.

Admittedly, it is hard for the EPA to make new laws, because the process for restricting chemical use under the Toxic Substances Control Act (TSCA) can take decades. The companies have around 7 years to stop using the chemical that is harmful and are given another 5 extra years if the company wishes to extend their time. Moreover, the Environmental Protection Agency that "administers TSCA, often works with companies on voluntary phase-out programs—which also take years to complete—as it has with the flame retardants known as polybrominated diphenyl ethers or PBDEs" [5]. We must be more vocal about making these changes sooner rather than later.

And yet, individual states and lobbyists can certainly take action as well. For instance, California did pass their own state law in order to regulate the use of chemicals, and in June, legislation was sent to President Barack Obama in order to get his signature approving the expanded power of the EPA. Passing new laws and increasing understanding of the impact pesticides are having on bees should be done immediately so that the EPA can better control chemical usage and provide safer environment for us, and the insects that help pollinate our planet, to live in [6].

Moreover, the latest version of the law, recently passed in June (No: 114–182.), grants the EPA greater power to examine the effects of around 2,000 chemicals. The EPA now also has the final say over decisions made by states. It seems that government is making huge progress, until one figures out that the government is not funding the EPA to carry out all the examinations. "The bill doesn't provide EPA enough money to get through this enormous backlog of old, and in some cases, very dangerous chemicals to assess whether they need to be regulated or even banned," said Scott Faber, vice president of government affairs at the Environmental Working Group, taking the EPA "decades to get through the thousand most dangerous chemicals that EPA itself has said need urgent review" (Scialla, (2016, June 22)). It seems like there are still many steps that the government has to take, although hopefully these are measures that will lead to far-reaching solution.

1. Greenpeace Research Laboratories Technical Report (Review) 01/2013
2. Voeller, D., & Nieh, J. (n.d.). Why are bees ecologically important?
3. Hagopian, J. (2016, March 07)
4. Williams, G. R., Troxler, A., Retschnig, G., Roth, K., Yañez, O., Shutler, D.
5. Gauthier, L. (2015, July 23)
6. Grossman, Elizabeth (2014, June 9 Li)
7. Hawthorn, Michael (2016, June 21)

Ⓥ **Assignment 1**: This article was written by a student for the *National High School Journal of Science.* It illustrates the work that high school students like yours can produce. Divide your students into small discussion groups of 3–4 students. Based on what your students learned in Chapters 1 and 2, have them discuss any errors in style they find in the essay above. Have each group answer and complete the following: Who is the audience? Why do you think that to be the case? Do you think the writer considered audience? Why or why not? Using bullet points, describe the errors your group found and be ready to share with the whole class.

Finally, have each group revise the sentences and paragraphs for clarity, conciseness, correctness, and readability. Have your students add more headings and descriptive headings to reveal the content more clearly. (Readers do not tolerate dense material!)

Ⓥ **Assignment 1A**: Many journals have limits on articles submitted. Revise this article to about half its length. Include a concise introduction designed to interest readers and develop a paragraph for each heading. What other ways can you make this article more concise and readable?

> ✓ **Assignment 1B**: How helpful do you and your students find the graphic? Explain what the graphic means. Readers make their decision on how much they read by reading the title, then the headings, and then the graphics. Can you think of a better word than "crop" for people seeing this article for the first time? Write a summary of the visual.

Example 3.2:

Veterinary Medicine's Increasing Role in Global Health
The Lancet, Volume 2, Issue 7, e379–e380, July 2014.

Thirteen zoonoses are responsible for a staggering 2.2 billion human illnesses and 2.3 million deaths per year, mostly in low-income and middle-income countries [Figure 3.2] where the correlation between rates of protein malnutrition and incidence of endemic zoonotic diseases is 99%. [1], [2] Veterinary medicine has an increasingly important role in global health, food security, and the post-2015 development goals proposed by a high level UN panel. [3] Three of the five proposed goals (ending all forms of extreme poverty; sustainable social, economic, and environmental development; and forging of a new global partnership connecting poverty relief with sustainable development) are unattainable without effective animal health services. Together with the livestock sector in general, [4] these services have been marginalised and underfunded for decades throughout much of the developing world to the point that they do not have the capacity to meet the challenges of an increasingly commercialised livestock industry, poverty relief, sustainable food security, and food safety.[4]–[6] For example, in 2013, hundreds of pigs that had died from unknown causes were dumped into a tributary of the Shanghai river, the source of much of Shanghai's drinking water. [7] This incident was symptomatic of larger problems with animal health care in China and prompted Jia Youling, head of the Chinese Veterinary Medical Association and former head of the Ministry of Agriculture's Bureau of Veterinary Medicine, to observe that the Chinese veterinary medical system is nowhere near adequate. Jia further remarked that in China, veterinary medicine is barely recognised as a profession. [7] Driven by rising urban wealth, escalating demand for foods of animal origin, and rising prices, livestock and poultry production are global agriculture's fastest growing industries. [8] Much of the growth is occurring in large-scale intensive operations, but escalating demand provides subsistence farmers with an unprecedented opportunity for economic growth and poverty reduction.

For more than 20 years, a global crisis in the emergence and transmission of zoonotic diseases from wildlife has been growing steadily, including severe acute respiratory syndrome, highly pathogenic avian influenza, Rift Valley fever, West Nile virus infection, Ebola haemorrhagic fever, Nipah virus infections, and Middle East respiratory syndrome. [9]–[11] Rapid expansion in food animal populations is also responsible for the emergence and spread of many human infections. Because emergent or reemerging zoonoses and many endemic zoonoses are not under satisfactory control, the absence of competent veterinary services is a cause for alarm. Other factors such as climate change, globalisation of world trade (including increased trade in animals and animal foodstuffs between developing nations), rapid movement of people around the globe, and encroachment of livestock farming into wildlife areas influence the dynamics of zoonotic disease spread and transmission. 75% of people in poverty live in rural areas [12] and more than 85% of livestock keepers in sub-Saharan Africa live in extreme poverty. [13] In such communities, hotspots of endemic disease trap people in poverty and pose a threat to the rest of the world. [1]

Disease control measures accompanied by opportunities for economic growth need to focus first on hotspots of endemic disease. Furthermore, because global food insecurity will be very expensive to counteract, increased production by the millions of subsistence livestock farmers in the world should be encouraged. At present, yields from their animals are meagre at best,

Figure 3.2

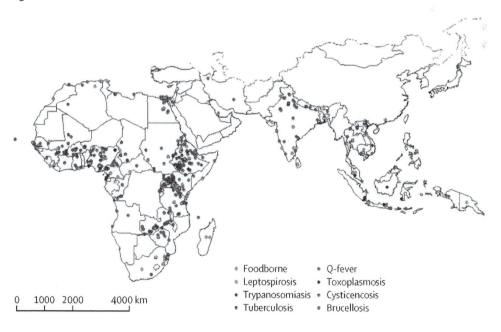

0   1000 2000   4000 km

• Foodborne   • Q-fever
• Leptospirosis   • Toxoplasmosis
• Trypanosomiasis • Cysticencosis
• Tuberculosis   • Brucellosis

owing to poor nutrition and chronic infections. Unhealthy livestock also carry increased food safety risks and restrict access to lucrative markets. As a result of these problems, more animals are needed to meet rising demand, which is not a sustainable approach. [14] A better approach would involve fewer, healthier, and more productive animals. Investment in research on infectious disease control and food safety is urgently needed in addition to studies on genetics, nutrition, management, market access, and rural economic growth. Beneficial interventions will require collaboration between medical, veterinary, agricultural, social, environmental, and wildlife scientists. Veterinary medicine intersects with all of these disciplines and for years has promoted the concept of One Health [15] as a technique for promotion of collaboration. The One Health Initiative, strengthened by the UN expert panel's recommendations, is slowly gathering momentum as the association between the health of all types of animals and poverty relief became more fully recognised. The challenges, however, remain daunting.

Alan Kelly, Bennie Osburn, Mo Salman School of Veterinary Medicine, University of Pennsylvania, Philadelphia, PA, USA (AK); School of Veterinary Medicine, University of California, Davis, CA, USA (BO); and College of Veterinary Medicine and Biomedical Science, Colorado State University, and Jefferson Sciences Fellow, Department of State, Washington, DC, USA (MS) kellya@vet.upenn.edu We declare no competing interests. Copyright © Kelly et al. Open Access article distributed under the terms of CC BY.

1. Grace D, Mutua F, Ochungo P, et al. Mapping of poverty and likely zoonoses hotspots. Report to the UK Department for International Development. http://cgspace.cgiar.org/handle/10568/21161 (accessed April 9, 2014).
2. Gilbert N. Cost of human-animal disease greatest for world's poor. http://www.nature.com/news/cost-of-human-animal-disease-greatest-forworld-s-poor-1.10953 (accessed April 9, 2014).
3. High Level Panel. The post-2015 development agenda. www.post2015hlp.org/ (accessed April 9, 2014).
4. Kelly A, Ferguson J, Galligan D, Salman M, Osburn B. One health, food security, and veterinary medicine. J Am Vet Med Assoc 2013; 242: 739–43.
5. Graham TW, Turk J, McDermott J, Brown C. Preparing veterinarians for work in resource-poor settings. J Am Vet Med Assoc 2013; 243: 1523–28.
6. Sherman DM. Tending animals in the global village: a guide to international veterinary medicine. Philadelphia: Lippincott Williams & Wilkins, 2002: 305–51.
7. Xu N. Shanghai pig scandal shows Chinese veterinary system is failing. https://www.chinadialogue.net/article/show/single/en/5873-Shanghaipig-scandal-shows-Chinese-veterinary-system-is-failing (accessed April 9, 2014).

8. Delgado C. Rising consumption of meat and milk has created a new food revolution. J Nutr 2003; 133 (suppl 2): S3907–10.
9. Food and Agriculture Organization of the UN. Changing disease landscapes, surge in diseases of animal origin necessitates new approach to health. www.fao.org/news/story/en/item/210621/icode/ (accessed May 21, 2014).
10. Jones K, Patel N, Levy M, et al. Global trends in emerging infectious diseases. Nature 451: 990–93.
11. Gibbs P. The evolution of one health: a decade of progress and challenges for the future. Vet Rec 2014; 174: 85–91.
12. Otte J, Upton M. Poverty and livestock agriculture. http://books.google. com/books?hl=en&lr=&id=0_3CegomgG4C&oi=fnd&pg=PA281&dq=Otte,+J.+Upton,+M+Poverty+and+Livestock+agriculture&ots=Vjt (accessed May 21, 2014).
13. Otte J, Costales A, Dijkman J, et al. Pro-Poor Livestock Policy Initiative: a living from livestock. www.fao.org/ag/againfo/programmes/en/ pplpi/home.html (accessed April 12, 2014).
14. Herrero M, Thornton P. Livestock and global change: Emerging issues for sustainable food systems. Proc Natl Acad Sci USA 2013; 110: 20878–81. 1
15. American Veterinary Medical Association. One health—it's all connected. https://www.avma.org/KB/Resources/Reference/Pages/One-Health.aspx (accessed April 9, 2014).

✔ **Assignment 1**: Note that this perspective article on veterinary medicine, from *The Lancet*, uses fairly clear language—devoid of excessive science jargon—and relatively short topic sentences that prepare readers for the content that follows. However, the article sorely needs **paragraphing, shorter paragraphs, and more condensation!** Ask your students to revise the article to improve readability by including headings. Have them create a topic sentence for each paragraph and shorten the opening paragraph.

✔ **Assignment 2**: (to be completed after covering Chapter 4): Assign your students to work in pairs. Have them take on the role of recruiting agents for the Texas A&M Veterinary School. In that role, they have been asked to give a six-minute presentation to high school juniors who have expressed interest in animal science. Each pair of recruiters must prepare a convincing presentation on the valuable role of veterinaries from the above article. Presentations will be given to the rest of the class.

When the Zika virus, first emerging in 1947, began to spread and reveal its damaging effects to the human fetus, articles in science journals and even newspapers carried coverage of the virus and its damage. The titles and the photos brought Zika front and center to U.S. readers. Articles and science letters began to appear in newspapers and science journals. Their goal: to provide information efficiently and readably to warn women about the danger of Zika to the unborn child and the possible relationship of climate change to the spread of Zika.

The next three examples focus on this disease and its still-emerging effects. Note that in all science writing, sources used are always cited, including any conflict of interest based on financial contributions from pharmaceutical or other companies. Note that this correspondence recognizes the horrors of Zika. And as the *Washington Post* article states, "The more we learn, the worse things seem to get."

Example 3.3:

Zika Outbreak: 'The More We Learn, the Worse Things Seem to Get'
By Lena H. Sun—Reprinted with Permission. *The Washington Post*, November 16, 2016

The top U.S. health officials leading response to the Zika virus, now sweeping through the hemisphere, have linked the mosquito-caused disease to a broad array of birth defects and neurological disorders worse than originally suspected.

Until Zika, stated Thomas Frieden, director of the Centers for Disease Control and Prevention, said Thursday during a conference call with reporters "we have never seen a mosquito-borne virus that could cause serious defects on such a large scale."

Frieden and Anthony Fauci, director of the National Institute of Allergy and Infectious Diseases, stated during Thursday's briefing that the need for federal funds to battle the disease remained urgent. They described the growing risk to pregnant women, the almost-certain link to Guillain-Barré syndrome, a neurological condition that can cause paralysis. The CDC has no effective agents to fight mosquitoes that have developed resistance to commonly used insecticides.

The speakers made clear that officials that they cannot lower expectations that they will be able to protect all pregnant women in the United States.

"There is nothing about Zika control that is quick or easy," Frieden said. "The only thing quick is the mosquito bite that can give it to you."

The *Aedes aegypti* mosquitoes which he saw at the Biomedical Sciences Institute in the Sao Paulo's University in Brazil, has Frieden "very concerned." The CDC director, who just returned from a trip to the island, said he expects hundreds of thousands of people will be infected by year's end, including thousands of pregnant women. The U.S. territory, on the "front lines of the battle, will increase not just steadily but dramatically," he said.

"That's an alarming finding and shows the negative impact on the fetus even if the mother is infected later on in pregnancy," he acknowledged.

We have increasingly strong evidence linking the virus to microcephaly: children are born with abnormally small heads and underdeveloped brains. The rare condition has surfaced in hundreds of babies in Brazil, the epicenter of a Zika outbreak that has spread to three dozen countries and territories, primarily in the Americas.

U.S. efforts underway attempt to develop a vaccine and new technologies to control mosquitoes and monitor and protect pregnant women and their babies. But those efforts cannot be sustained over the long term without the $1.9 billion in emergency funding sought by the Obama administration, according to Frieden and Fauci. Congress has balked at approving the request.

With the approach of the rainy season in Puerto Rico and warmer temperatures in the rest of the United States, Frieden and Fauci said that it is critical that the emergency funding be approved. For now, the CDC and NIH have been moving resources from existing programs. The CDC has about 750 of its staff working

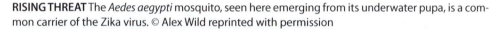

RISING THREAT The *Aedes aegypti* mosquito, seen here emerging from its underwater pupa, is a common carrier of the Zika virus. © Alex Wild reprinted with permission

Zika Babies

Photos from Yahoo Babies

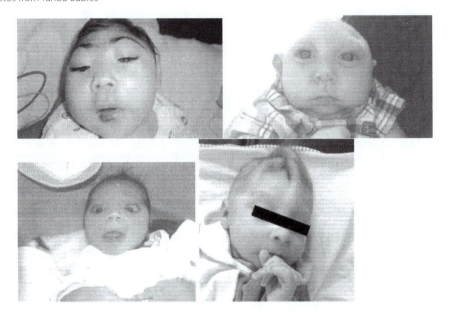

full-time on Zika. That number includes its Dengue Branch in Puerto Rico, which has shifted from dengue, a related virus the leading cause of illness and death in the tropics and subtropics. The agency's Fort Collins, Colorado, office also has stopped working on some new tick-borne viruses to focus on Zika, Frieden said.

"We are scraping together every dime we can to respond to this," Frieden said. "It is definitely interfering with our ability to mount a robust response. . . . and affecting our ability to protect Americans from other health threats."

At the NIH, the researchers trying to accelerate a Zika vaccine are part of a team also developing vaccines for flu, the AIDS virus, and respiratory syncytial virus, the most common germ causing infections in infants and young children.

"There may be a point where we have to slow down at least one or maybe all three of those until we can get money," Fauci said. "It's a give and take. . . . You have to slow down or stop. We try very hard not to stop things."

The cost of caring for one child with birth defects can be $10 million or more, Frieden said. Frieden also said a misperception also exists that Puerto Ricans are not that concerned about the virus because the island has had outbreaks from dengue and chikungunya, related viruses carried by the same mosquito species.

"That is not the case," he said. "Every pregnant woman we met had a high degree of awareness and concern," he said. He remembered one in particular, who was fearful of what would happen to her baby. She said, "I will be worried for my whole life, and even after I die, who is going to take care of the baby," he recalled.

Health authorities in Puerto Rico are working with the CDC to identify pregnant women most at risk—those living in parts of the island where there is active transmission—and provide window screens for their homes.

But an initial test installing screens in some apartments highlighted the difficulties going forward. Some homes have open eaves, so screens would have little or no impact. Other residents were reluctant to have window screens because they feared the screens would restrict air flow and raise indoor temperatures.

Puerto Rico has about 160 confirmed Zika infections. Another 193 cases have been confirmed in the mainland from people getting bitten in Zika-affected areas; they include six where travelers passed the virus to partners through sex.

On Capitol Hill, Republican appropriators have so far refused to approve emergency funding for Zika. In a Feb. 18 letter, they pointed to roughly $2.7 billion in unspent Ebola response funds that could be redirected to Zika efforts.

"If the aim of the request is to mount as rapid a response as possible, it is clear to us that the most expeditious way to identify the needed funding is to maximize the use of unobligated funds previously provided for Ebola response, prevention, and preparedness," the top House lawmakers wrote. If additional funds are needed, they said, they could be considered as part of the fiscal 2017 spending program.

Example 3.4:

Zika Virus: Ethics Preparedness for Old and New Challenges
Carla Saenz, *The Lancet Global Health*, Volume 4, Issue 10, e686, October 2016.

In its July editorial, *The Lancet Global Health* drew attention to the ethical challenges posed by the Zika virus outbreak. [1] The Regional Program on Bioethics at the Pan American Health Organization (PAHO) arranged an ethics consultation, funded by the Wellcome Trust, to provide ethically sound guidance for the outbreak. Ethicists—mostly from the Americas—and other professionals involved in the response analysed the ethical issues that affected countries had identified as most challenging, and developed ethics guidance for health-care delivery, public health, and research. [2]

Some challenges in Zika virus ethics are new. For the first time, a mosquito-borne virus infection has been shown to cause congenital malformations. [3] Despite growing evidence about the virus and its consequences, uncertainty and diagnostic challenges prevail. In this scenario, PAHO's Zika ethics guidance highlights the moral duty to give women of childbearing age up-to-date information, the capacity to choose between all relevant reproductive options, access to comprehensive reproductive health care, and social support.

Some of these challenges are, however, old. The difficulties of catalysing research during an emergency, distinguishing research from public health activities involving data collection, sharing data promptly, obtaining consent for research during an outbreak, handling uncertainty in communications, and setting priorities during an emergency were raised by the affected countries as most pressing. Yet reflection on these ethics issues has already taken place; for example, after the Ebola virus outbreak. [4]

PAHO's Zika ethics guidance addresses these issues. However, the discussion should continue on the reasons why the lessons that could have been learned are still posing challenges, and how to ensure that the same situation does not occur in a future outbreak.

Progress has certainly been made, encouraged by the Region of the America's 2012 commitment to integrate ethics in health care. [5] The Zika virus outbreak has led to further progress. PAHO's Zika ethics consultation has strengthened our capacity to do ethics analysis collectively and provide guidance for specific problems. Moreover, ethics is being embedded in other areas—e.g. in the support of PAHO's Latin American Center for Perinatology, Women and Reproductive Health to Ministries of Health to respond to the outbreak. [6]

In the midst of a health emergency, we should reinvigorate the commitment to integrate ethics in health care. [1] This integration is not a job to be left only to bioethicists. We must all take action now, strengthen our ethics preparedness, and ensure that work in health care is always ethically sound.

I declare no competing interests.

I gratefully acknowledge the comments of Ludovic Reveiz (PAHO), Rodolfo Gómez Ponce de León (PAHO), and John F Tisdale (NIH) to a previous version of this letter. The views expressed are those of CS and do not necessarily reflect the official opinions or policies of PAHO or Wellcome Trust.

References
1. The Lancet Global Health. The right(s) approach to Zika. *Lancet Global Health*, 4 (2016), p. e427.
2. Pan American Health Organization. *Zika ethics consultation: ethics guidance on key issues raised by the outbreak*. Washington, DC: Pan American Health Organization, 2016.
3. B Miranda-Filho Dde, CM Martelli, RA Ximenes, *et al*. Initial description of the presumed congenital Zika syndrome. *American Journal of Public Health*, 106 (2016), pp. 598–600.
4. Global Forum on Bioethics in Research. *Meeting report: emerging epidemic infections and experimental medical treatments*; Annecy, France; Nov 3–4, 2015. www.gfbr.global/wp-content/uploads/2016/03/GFBR-2015-meeting-

report-emerging-epidemic-infections-and-experimental-medical-treatments.pdf (accessed July 28, 2016).

5. Pan American Health Organization Directing Council. *Bioethics: towards the integration of ethics in health*. Concept paper. 28th Pan American Sanitary Conference, 64th Session of the Regional Committee; Washington, DC, USA; Sept 17–21, 2012 (CSP28/14, Rev.1). http://new.paho.org/hq/index.php?option=com_docman&task=doc_download&gid=18416&Itemid=&lang=en (accessed July 28, 2016).

6. Pan American Health Organization. *The region makes a commitment on access to modern contraceptives in the context of the Zika virus alert*. www.paho.org/clap/index.php?option=com_content&view=article&id=389:the-region-makes-a-commitment-on-access-to-modern-contraceptives-in-the-context-of-the-zika-virus-alert&catid=387&Itemid=354&lang=en (accessed July 28, 2016).

Example 3.5:

The Right(s) Approach to Zika
The Lancet Global Health, Volume 4, Issue 7, e427, July 2016.

The Zika virus epidemic is spreading. 63 countries are now reporting transmission, over 1500 cases of related microcephaly or CNS malformations have been confirmed this year, and knowledge on the disease is advancing slowly. Adding to the tension around Zika, at the epicentre of the outbreak, Brazil braces for a large-scale mass gathering: the Olympic and Paralympic Games 2016 in Rio de Janeiro. Conflicting opinions on the need to postpone or cancel the Games have been expressed, but during the 69th World Health Assembly last month, the WHO issued clear public health advice on the matter: the Games will not significantly change the international spread of the virus, and travellers can reduce their risk of contracting the disease by following simple prevention measures such as avoiding mosquito bites with repellents and adequate clothing, practising safe sex, staying in air-conditioned housing, and avoiding areas with poor water and sanitation. These recommendations are sound and reasonable. They also highlight the true nature of Zika: it is a disease of the poor and disenfranchised.

The face of Zika is not often seen in the airconditioned shopping malls of upscale Rio neighbourhoods or on the beaches of Ipanema. Rio has its fair share of cases, but so far the heaviest burden has been borne by the northeast region of Brazil, where poverty, poor infrastructure, and lack of access to health services are rampant, and the penetration of *Aedes aegypti* is high. A large proportion of the population in that region is of African descent—indeed, the face of Zika is often that of a darker-skinned person. And because most cases are asymptomatic, and the most dramatic signs of the disease appear through congenital Zika syndrome, the face of Zika is that of a woman or a small child. That is at least what we are able to outline, because in spite of the need for disaggregated epidemiological data to understand transmission patterns and evaluate interventions in vulnerable populations, we have no reliable count of Zika cases by sex and ethnicity. Last month, *The Lancet Global Health* published WHO's interim guidance on pregnancy management in the context of Zika virus infection. The guidance includes recommendations for preventing and managing infection in pregnant women. Vector control is emphasised, as well as personal protection such as clothing, bednets, repellents, and safe sex. Again these are sound recommendations, duly relayed by health authorities, but they certainly don't resonate in the poorest neighbourhoods of Brazil and other affected countries, where the availability, practicality, and affordability of protective items are doubtful and where safe sex is not always negotiable. When prevention fails, other issues surface: information, lack of access to basic services and diagnostic tests, and most importantly a blatant lack of choice.

So in spite of the intensifying efforts of civil society, UN agencies, and national authorities to address these issues—controlling vectors, launching communication campaigns, planning for long-term child services—this is where poor women in Brazil, Colombia, El Salvador, and elsewhere have been let down by their governments. They are at the centre of the epidemics, they are scrutinised and lectured, but lack of access to basic reproductive services and restrictive abortion laws have stripped them of a choice when faced with the dire consequences of the virus on their health and that of their children. This imbalance has been recognised and is being acted upon, in Brazil in particular, where a group of lawyers, academics, and activists is bringing a case in front of the Supreme Court to request, among other things, access to information, to health services, and to safe abortions for victims of Zika. In early April, the Pan American Health Organization issued a guidance document on the key ethical issues raised by the epidemic that echo those demands and include the duty of all governments to provide information, respect the right to choose, and provide access to comprehensive reproductive health care and social support to women affected by Zika and their children. In many ways, Zika is the epitome of the interdependence of health and human rights. Controlling vectors is an essential step, but it will be ineffectual without a rights-centred approach.

The Lancet Global Health
Copyright © The Lancet Global Health Published by Elsevier

✓ **Assignment 1**: Your students have been asked to write a short—700 words or less—report on the Zika virus for the district parent newsletter. Using the information provided in the reports in Examples 3.3, 3.4, and 3.5, have each student write an article for submission. You may want to search for a real publication source for this assignment. Recommend a database where students can search for more information.

The title of an article is critical because it must interest readers. Ask your students how the titles in Examples 3.3–3.5 interest readers. Ask them if they find paragraphs that could be shortened. Let them use those observations as they write their own reports.

✓ **Assignment 2**: Have your students compare and contrast two of the Zika papers presented in Examples 3.3, 3.4, and 3.5. Students should note the intended audiences, how the material was presented, and the purpose. Students may have to use a pharmaceutical dictionary in your library or do computer research to translate in parentheses the meanings of the medical terms.

Example 3.6:
The Lancet, Volume 2, No. 5, e251–e252, May 2014

Reassessing the Value of Vaccines

◆ Till Bärnighausen[a, b],
◆ Seth Berkley[c],
◆ Zulfiqar A Bhutta[d, e],
◆ David M Bishai[g],
◆ Maureen M Black[h],
◆ David E Bloom[b],
◆ Dagna Constenla[g],
◆ Julia Driessen[i],
◆ John Edmunds[j],
◆ David Evans[k],
◆ Ulla Griffiths[j],
◆ Peter Hansen[c],
◆ Farah Naz Hashmani[f],
◆ Raymond Hutubessy[k],
◆ Dean T Jamison[l],

◆ Prabhat Jha[m],
◆ Mark Jit[j, n],
◆ Hope Johnson[c],
◆ Ramanan Laxminarayan[o],
◆ Bruce Y Lee[p],
◆ Sharmila Mhatre[q],
◆ Anne Mills[j],
◆ Anders Nordström[r],
◆ Sachiko Ozawa[p],
◆ Lisa Prosser[s],
◆ Karlee Silver[t],
◆ Christine Stabell Benn[u],
◆ Baudouin Standaert[v],
◆ Damian Walker[w]

In May, 1974, WHO launched the Expanded Programme on Immunization—the global programme to immunise children worldwide with a set of (at the time) six core vaccines. 40 years on, the GAVI Alliance has brought us together, a group of 29 leading technical experts in health and development economics, cognitive development, epidemiology, disease burden, and economic modelling to review and understand the broader outcomes of vaccines beyond morbidity and mortality, to identify research opportunities, and to create a research agenda that will help to further quantify the value of this effect.

What is the value of immunizing every child with all 11 vaccines that WHO now recommends, [1] beyond the prevention of illness and death? The full benefits of childhood vaccination could reach well into a child's life, through adulthood, into the wider community, and, ultimately, the national economy. [2] Some evidence of these benefits has already been generated, but gaps in knowledge remain.

For example, preliminary research suggests that a 5-year improvement in life expectancy can translate into 0.3–0.5% more annual growth added to income per head. [3] Similarly, results of research done in Bangladesh show that the benefits of antibodies from maternal tetanus vaccinations passing from a mother to her unborn child can lead to gains of about 0.25 years of schooling for children whose parents did not attend school. [4] And findings from the Philippines showed that vaccinations induced improvements in test scores in children, [5] which had a return on investment as high as 21% when translated into the earning gains of adults. [6]

Meanwhile in South Africa, researchers have shown a significant association between overage of measles vaccination and the level of school-grade attainment in sibling-pairs, after controlling for intrinsic factors such as birth order, education levels of parents, and household wealth. [7] This research suggests that, on average, 1 year of schooling is gained for every six children vaccinated against measles. But evidence to link health inputs and wealth outcomes needs to be further assessed and investigated.

Vaccines are usually given when the rate of brain development is at its peak, which can benefit cognitive development through prevention of illness and its neurological complications (e.g., encephalitis). But so far, the only evidence for this model is based on observational studies; such studies are an important first step, but more work is needed. Similarly, evidence for the positive links between vaccines and the educational attainment of children, or how improvements in child survival can lead to lower fertility rates, exists but needs more elaboration.

Similarly, evidence exists for links between improvements in survival, cognition, physical capacity, and educational attainment, and increases in workforce supply and productivity. [8] How reductions in mortality and morbidity can boost consumption and gross domestic product (GDP) can be modelled, but to understand these links better, more research is needed.

Although it follows logically that vaccination can prevent disease and therefore reduce health-care costs, more evidence is needed. This is also the case for evidence that links loss of productivity with specific diseases. We have some evidence, but the picture remains incomplete. Follow-up studies for education and income are needed. For expediency, these studies could be done through follow-up of previous randomised controlled trials and through investigators finding clever ways to add these questions onto prospective studies, such as studies embedded in health and demographic surveillance sites.

As well as generating new data, it is important to obtain and mine data from previous studies of existing vaccines used in the Expanded Programme on Immunization. Similarly, the links between productivity and specific diseases could be made clearer through the addition of economic or other quantitative socioeconomic analyses to clinical trials of new vaccines, such as those against dengue and malaria. Also, the need for different metrics to measure the effectiveness of vaccines could be met by the use of economic approaches that include broader measures of wellbeing, such as willingness to pay and value of statistical life. [2] These measures are by no means perfect and are not straightforward to interpret when applied to childhood vaccination. One of the difficulties in interpretation is that it can be problematic to separate the effect of vaccinations from other health-care interventions during assessment of costs and benefits.

Clearly, much work still needs to be done, but the potential rewards are huge. Two studies have already been commissioned by GAVI to try to fill these gaps—one in Nigeria will explore issues of equity and trust (these issues can play a part in the overall effect and coverage of vaccines); the other will look for new evidence of economic benefits with vaccination in India. However, GAVI is not a research organisation. The main drive must come from the broader academic community and not simply organisations traditionally concerned with vaccines.

Mortality reduction is already reason enough to have every child on this planet fully immunised, as shown by the Millennium Development Goals and the post-2015 development agenda. Now this fight is not simply about saving lives, but about maximising the full lifetime potential of these children and the economic health of the families

We declare that we have no competing interests and countries in which authors live.

References

1. WHO. *Summary of WHO position papers—recommendations for routine immunization*. www.who.int/immunization/policy/Immunization_routine_table1.pdf?ua=1 (accessed April 7, 2014).

2. DT Jamison, LH Summers, G Alleyne, *et al*. Global health 2035: a world converging within a generation. *Lancet*, 382 (2013), pp. 1898–1955

3. DE Bloom, D Canning. The health and wealth of nations. *Science*, 287 (2000), pp. 1207–1209

4. D Canning, A Razzaque, J Driessen, DG Walker, PK Streatfield, M Yunus. The effect of maternal tetanus immunization on 'children's schooling attainment in Matlab, Bangladesh: follow-up of a randomized trial. *Social Science & Medicine*, 72 (2011), pp. 1429–1436

5. DE Bloom, D Canning, ES Shenoy. The effect of vaccination on children's physical and cognitive development in the Philippines. *Applied Economics*, 44 (2012), pp. 2777–2783

6. DE Bloom. The value of vaccination. *Advances in Experimental Medicine and Biology*, 697 (2011), pp. 1–8

7. T Anekwe, M Newell, T Bärnighausen. *The impact of measles vaccination on educational attainment in rural KwaZulu-Natal*. GAVI Alliance Value of Vaccines Meeting; Annecy, France; Jan 14–15, 2013.

8. R Deogaonkar, R Hutubessy, I van der Putten, S Evers, M Jit. Systematic review of studies evaluating the broader economic impact of vaccination in low and middle income countries. *BMC Public Health*, 12 (2012), p. 878

Assignment 1: Before you have your students read the article on vaccines, ask them what effect the long list of authors has on them. How do paragraph length and topic sentences affect readability?

Assignment 2: Assign your students to research a database. Look for the key word "vaccination." What attitudes do they see expressed about vaccinations? Ask your students to write a convincing report based on their findings answering the question, "Should vaccinations be required for all children?" Which vaccinations should be required? You may want them to prepare a PowerPoint presentation to an audience of their choice to accompany their report. Suggestion: Have students include a heading that includes the name of the disease for which each vaccine is required as a development guide for the report.

Assignment 3: Make a class list of what your students already know or believe about vaccines.

Example 3.7:

Trends in Diabetes: Sounding the Alarm
Etienne G King, *The Lancet*, 9–15. April 2016

Diabetes is a major cause of death and disability worldwide. In 2012 it caused as many deaths as HIV/AIDS (1.5 million).[1]

Disability resulting from diabetes has grown substantially since 1990, with particularly large increases among people aged 15–69 years.[2]

People with all types of diabetes are at risk of developing a range of complications that can endanger their health and survival, and the high costs of care increase the risk of catastrophic medical expenditure.[3]

Diabetes is the theme of this year's World Health Day on April 7, and WHO has published the Global Report on Diabetes to raise awareness and spark momentum for action at the necessary scale.

In The Lancet, the NCD Risk Factor Collaboration (NCD-RisC) [4] presents a robust and timely analysis of trends in diabetes prevalence. They provide updated, consistent, and comparable estimates of age-standardised prevalence of diabetes since 1980, derived from 751 population-based measurement studies involving nearly 44 million participants. These are the first global estimates and trend analyses published since adoption of the voluntary target to halt the rise in diabetes and obesity (against the 2010 baseline) by 2025.

The news is not good. NCD-RisC estimates that the number of people with diabetes quadrupled between 1980 and 2014. Age-standardised prevalence among adult men doubled during that time (from 4.3% [95% credible interval 2.4–7.0] to 9.0% [7.2–11.1]), and age-standardised prevalence among adult women increased by 60% (5.0% [2.9–7.9] to 7.9% [6.4–9.7]). Diabetes prevalence either increased or remained the same in every country. Given these trends, the authors calculate that only a few countries, mostly in western Europe, have even a chance of meeting the target to halt the rise in diabetes by 2025—a sobering wake-up call. With diabetes in the World Health Day spotlight the question is, how will the world and its leaders respond to the alarm?

NCD-RisC notes that reducing the global health and economic impact of diabetes requires action to prevent or delay the onset of type 2 diabetes, which accounts for the majority of diabetes worldwide. Overweight and obesity, together with physical inactivity, are responsible for a substantial proportion of the global diabetes burden.**5**

Changes at population level to improve access to healthy foods and beverages, and to opportunities for physical activity, facilitate positive behavioural change and are likely to have an impact on the occurrence of type 2 diabetes.**6**

References
1. WHO. Fact sheet no 310; the top 10 causes of death, updated May 2014, *World Health Organization, Geneva* (2015).
2. Global Burden of Disease Study 2013 Collaborators. Global, regional, and national incidence, prevalence, and years lived with disability for 301 acute and chronic diseases and injuries in 188 countries, 1990–2013: a systematic analysis for the *Global Burden of Disease Study* 2013. *Lancet*, 386 (2015), pp. 743–800.
3. CM1 Smith-Spangler, J Bhattacharya, JD Goldhaber-Fiebert. Diabetes, its treatment, and catastrophic medical spending in 35 developing countries. *Diabetes Care*, 35 (2012), pp. 319–326.
4. NCD Risk Factor Collaboration (NCD-RisC). Worldwide trends in diabetes since 1980: a pooled analysis of 751 population-based studies with 4·4 million participants. *Lancet* (2016) published online April 6. http://dx.doi.org.ezproxy.library.tamu.edu/10.1016/S0140-6736(16)00618-8
5. GBD 2013 Risk Factors Collaborators. Global, regional, and national comparative risk assessment of 79 behavioural, environmental and occupational, and metabolic risks or clusters of risks in 188 countries, 1990–2013: a systematic analysis for the *Global Burden of Disease Study* 2013. *Lancet*, 386 (2015), pp. 2287–2323.
6. WHO. Global report on diabetes, *World Health Organization, Geneva* (2016). http://www.sciencedirect.com.ezproxy.library.tamu.edu/science/article/pii/S0140673616301635

> ✅ **Assignment 1**: Diabetes is prevalent everywhere. After discussing this technical letter, ask students to identify someone with diabetes whom they can interview. Their assignment should be to write a science letter titled *Living with Diabetes* that includes the individual's family history of the disease, the symptoms that led to the discovery that they had diabetes, how the disease impacts their life, what life changes have they had to make, and how difficult those changes were. Finally, what advice would they give to young people to avoid getting diabetes?

> ✅ **Assignment 2**: Have students write a short article about the prevalence of diabetes. Why has diabetes increased so rapidly? What can be done? Again, have them consult a database for articles about the diabetes problem.

Example 3.8:

Beyond Ebola: Lessons to Mitigate Future Pandemics
The Lancet, Volume 3, No. 7, e354–e355, July 2015

It is now just more than a year since the official confirmation of an outbreak of Ebola haemorrhagic fever in west Africa. [1] With new cases occurring at their lowest rate for 2015, [2] and the end of the outbreak in sight for all three countries predominantly affected, now is the time to consider strategies to prevent future outbreaks of this, and other, zoonotic pathogens. The Ebola outbreak, like many other emerging diseases, illustrates the crucial role of the ecological, social, political, and economic context within which diseases emerge. Increasing anthropogenic environmental changes, coupled with a globalized network of travel and trade, allow zoonotic pathogens to spill over into human beings with increasing frequency, and leave us supremely vulnerable to their international spread. [3]

Pandemics are no longer simply the domain of public health and clinical medicine, but are a social issue, a development issue, and a global security issue. The cost of management of infectious disease outbreaks is almost always greater than the cost of avoiding them. For severe acute respiratory syndrome (SARS), the global cost of a single outbreak was estimated to be between US$13 billion and US$50 billion at the currency values of the 2003 outbreak. [4],[5] For Ebola, the cost might be higher—both in the direct, short-term cost of control, patient care, and hospital admission, and in the indirect, longer-term dislocation of the regional economies in west Africa. [6] The economic costs of disease emergence are projected to continue to rise in line with increasing frequency of outbreaks driven by expanding socioeconomic and environmental changes that cause diseases to emerge. [7] Migration of future pandemic threats such as Ebola is therefore more cost-effective than the current approach of emerging diseases, probably began with a zoonotic spillover from a wildlife reservoir, in this case thought to be bats. [10] Targeted programs for behavior change, focusing on incentives for bush meat hunting, should be part of the mitigation strategy.

This approach was trialed in central Africa, with education programs responding to outbreaks after they have begun to spread rapidly in the human population. [7] What would mitigation strategies to deal with future pandemic risks of zoonotic disease look like? Analyses of emerging disease trends during the past six decades have shown that Ebola fits the dominant pattern. [8] This pattern involves zoonotic spillover from wildlife or livestock driven by changes in land use, crop choices, migration patterns, animal husbandry, trade, transport, and travel. [9] The west African Ebola outbreak, similar to previous outbreaks of Ebola, HIV, SARS, influenza, and most other diseases designed to reduce the consumption of primates found dead in forests, and has been shown to offer a cost-effective way to mitigate the risk of an Ebola outbreak. [11] Additionally, projects aimed to reduce dependency on bush meat need to be supported, either through creative approaches to farming of some wildlife species, or by expansion of livestock production, with appropriate biosecurity and surveillance to prevent emergence of other zoonoses.

The acceleration of vaccine development for Ebola as part of an outbreak control strategy could also have a crucial role to mitigate future outbreaks. Ebola's propensity for nosocomial spread (noted in west Africa and in many previous Ebola outbreaks) could be curtailed by pre-outbreak vaccination of critical care workers in Ebola virus hotspots. Likewise, targeted training in infection control, and efforts to maintain surge capacity between outbreaks, will be crucial for rapid response to the first cases in a future emergence event.

Can these approaches be scaled up to mitigate future pandemics on a global scale? Global mitigation of future pandemic risk must focus on the large scale behaviors that lead to zoonotic spillovers. This approach means engaging with the sectors that drive disease emergence, including industries involved in land-use change, resource extraction, livestock production, travel, and trade, among others. Large economic development programs will need health impact assessments that deal explicitly with the risk of emergence of novel diseases, and plans to set up new clinics and surveillance programs listed as project deliverables. An improved understanding of the liability for disease emergence, will drive this change; when all are at risk, collective action is needed to strengthen the weakest links in the chain. [12],[13] Although existing multilateral agreements (e.g., the International Health Regulations) allow for some coordination of national responses to outbreaks and bilateral interventions to build public health capacity in poor countries, more is needed. Collective investment needs to occur through a mechanism similar to the Global Environment Faculty, not just in local public health infrastructure, but also in so-called one health measures to reduce the likelihood of zoonotic spillovers. Management of future risk will need anticipation of the origin and spread of diseases through improved predictive models of emergence that include animal populations, the powerful new drivers of global trade and travel, and the effect of disparities in income and wealth on health infrastructure, risk mitigation, presymptomatic diagnosis, and vaccination. [14],[15] Perhaps the biggest challenge is that the identity of future emerging diseases will often be unknown before emergence (e.g., as in SARS and HIV). Is it possible to design a strategy for an as-yet unknown pathogen? This task seems daunting, but it has already begun, partly though reduction of the size of the problem and allocation of resources in an objective way to the locations most at risk. Analysis of trends in disease emergence provides a strategy to identify the places most likely to propagate the next pandemic. [3] These hotspots for disease emergence tend to be tropical regions with high wildlife diversity that harbor known unknown zoonoses, and high levels of socioeconomic and environmental change. [3] USAID's Emerging Pandemic Threats (PREDICT) program targets these devastation when pandemics strike. hotspots to identify known and previously unknown viruses in wildlife species known to be zoonotic reservoirs, analyses patterns of high-risk human behavior, tests people for evidence of these viruses moving across the species barrier, and enables the design of strategies to reduce the risk of even the first spillover event. [8] Identification of the next Ebola virus, or the next HIV, will not be a simple task, but estimates of the diversity of viruses existing on the planet show that it is not impossible. [16] Surely this threat is worth concerted effort, given the human tragedy and economic effects.

*Carlos Castillo-Chavez, Roy Curtiss, *Peter Daszak,*
Simon A Levin, Oscar Patterson-Lomba, Charles Perrings,
George Poste, Sherry Towers

The Simon A Levin Mathematical, Computational and Modeling Sciences Center (CC-C, ST, SAL), Biodesign Institute (RC), School of Life Sciences (CP), and Arizona State University, Tempe, AZ, USA; EcoHealth Alliance, New York, NY10001, USA (PD); Department of Ecology and Evolutionary Biology, Princeton University, Princeton, NJ, USA (SAL); Department of Biostatistics, Harvard TH Chan School of Public Health, Boston, MA, USA (OP-L); and Complex Adaptive Systems Initiative, Arizona State University, Scottsdale, AZ, USA (GP)

daszak@ecohealthalliance.org
We declare no competing interests.

PD, OP-L, CP, and ST are funded by a Joint NSF-NIH-USDA/BBSRC Ecology and Evolution of Infectious Disease award (NSF DEB 1414374, BBSRC BB/M008894/1); CC-C, PD, SAL, OP-L, CP by an NIH (NIGMS) grant 1R01GM100471-01; PD by the US Agency for International Development (USAID) Emerging Pandemic Threats-PREDICT program; and OP-L by the NIH, grant T32AI007358-26.

1. WHO Regional Office for Africa. *Ebola virus disease in Guinea*, 2014. www.afro.who.int/en/clusters-a-programmes/dpc/epidemic-apandemic-alert-and-response/outbreak-news/4063-ebola-virus-diseasein-guinea.html (accessed March 25, 2015).
2. WHO. *Ebola situation reports*, 2015. http://apps.who.int/ebola/en/current-situation/ebola-situation-report (accessed March 25, 2015).
3. KE Jones, NG Patel, MA Levy, *et al*. Global trends in emerging infectious diseases. *Nature*, 451 (2008), pp. 990–994.
4. M Brahmbhatt, A Dutta. *On SARS type economic effects during infectious disease outbreaks*. Washington, DC: World Bank East Asia and Pacific Region, Chief Economist's Office, 2008.
5. P Beutels, N Jia, Q Zhou, R Smith, W Cao, S de Vlas. The economic impact of SARS in Beijing, China. *Tropical Medicine & International Health*, 14 (2009), pp. 85–91.
6. World Bank. *The economic impact of the 2014 Ebola epidemic: short and medium term estimates for West Africa*. Washington, DC: World Bank Group, 2014.
7. J Pike, TL Bogich, S Elwood, DC Finnoff, P Daszak. Economic optimization of a global stategy to reduce the pandemic threat. *Proceedings of the National Academy of Sciences of the United States of America*, 111 (2014), pp. 18519–18523.
8. SS Morse, JAK Mazet, M Woolhouse, *et al*. Prediction and prevention of the next pandemic zoonosis. *Lancet*, 380 (2012), pp. 1956–1965.
9. CR Janes, KK Corbett, JH Jones, J Trostle. Emerging infectious diseases: the role of social sciences. *Lancet*, 380 (2012), pp. 1884–1886.
10. A Marí Saéz, S Weiss, K Nowak, *et al*. Investigating the zoonotic origin of the West African Ebola epidemic. *EMBO Molecular Medicine*, 7 (2015), pp. 17–23.
11. WB Karesh. *Implementing urgent measures for the surveillance and protection of Great Apes in northern Congo in response to recent Ebola outbreaks: final report to U.S. Fish & Wildlife Service on grant number 98210-5-G195*. New York, NY: Wildlife Conservation Society, 2007.
12. C Perrings, M Williamson, EB Barbier, *et al*. Biological invasion risks and the public good: an economic perspective. *Conservation Ecology*, 6 (2002), pp. 155–179.

13. T Sandler. *Global collective action*. Cambridge: Cambridge University Press, 2004.
14. C Perrings, C Castillo-Chavez, G Chowell, *et al*. Merging economics and epidemiology to improve the prediction and management of infectious disease. *Ecohealth*, 11 (2014), pp. 464–475.
15. E Fenichel, C Castillo-Chavez, M Ceddia, *et al*. Adaptive human behavior in epidemiological models. *Proceedings of the National Academy of Sciences of the United States of America*, 108 (2011), pp. 6306–6311.
16. Anthony SJ, Epstein JH, Murray KA, *et al*. A strategy to estimate unknown viral diversity in mammals. *Mbio*, 4 (2013), p. e00598-13.

✓ **Assignment**: Ask your students to research Ebola in the area in which they live. The article in Example 3.8 states that "an Ebola outbreak, like many other emerging diseases, illustrates the crucial role of the ecological, social, political, and economic context within which diseases emerge." As an assignment, ask your students to write a short article on their findings, addressing the different contexts listed above.

Then, have your students identify a publication with an audience that would be interested in such an article and pursue getting their informative article published.

Have your students also read article from the *National High School Journal of Science* in Example 3.9. Ask them if the information about Ebola from this journal helps them develop their own article.

Example 3.9:

The Ebola Virus Had More Opportunities to Mutate During the West African Epidemic Than Ever Before

Has a New Mutation in the Ebola Virus Made It Deadlier?

NIAID, *National High School Journal of Science*
By Jon Cohen Nov. 3, 2016, 12:00 PM

The sheer size of the **Ebola epidemic** that began in 2013 and engulfed West Africa is still a bit of a riddle for scientists. Previous Ebola outbreaks had never

Figure 3.3 Ebola Virus

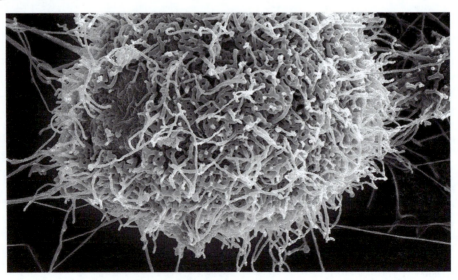

sickened more than 600 people. But the outbreak in Liberia, Sierra Leone, and Guinea infected more than 28,000 before it was finally brought under control. Part of the explanation was that the virus had suddenly surfaced in major cities, making it harder to stamp out than in the isolated rural locales where it had struck before. The countries' poor public health infrastructure and other environmental factors played roles as well.

But two papers raise another intriguing possibility. They show that some 3 months after the outbreak took off and became a full-blown epidemic, the virus underwent a mutation that made it better suited for humans than for its presumed natural host, a fruit bat species. "The virus has never had this many human-to-human transmissions before, and there are a lot of mutations happening," says Harvard University's Pardis Sabeti, an evolutionary geneticist who co-authored one of the papers.

Sabeti stresses that her team only has a "circumstantial" case about the timing of the mutation and the epidemic's explosion, but her group and an independent team that published the second study have amassed what she calls "compelling evidence" that for the first time links a mutation in the virus to a preference for human cells. The findings "raise the possibility that this mutation contributed directly to greater transmission and thus to the severity of the outbreak," the team writes. And they found an "association" with increased mortality. "We should neither be alarmist nor complacent," Sabeti says. "Any possibility that one of the mutations can have a serious impact should be interrogated."

Working with a team led by Jeremy Luban from the University of Massachusetts Medical School in Worcester, Sabeti and co-workers sequenced samples from 1489 West African patients and analyzed them. By March 2014—about the time the epidemic was detected, but some 3 months after the first case actually occurred—the sequences had split into two distinct lineages, one of which was characterized by a single amino acid change in a region of the virus's surface protein and allows it to bind to cells. The mutant, Luban says, "completely supplanted the ancestral virus."

The big question, of course, is whether the mutation could help the virus spread. The researchers did not have access to a biosafety level (BSL) 4 laboratory necessary to test that with the real Ebola virus, so they engineered harmless "pseudotyped" viruses that contained the gene for the surface protein in both its ancestral and mutated form. The mutant **far more easily infected human immune cells than did the ancestral pseudotype**, the team reports today in *Cell*. The researchers also showed that the mutant more easily infects primate cells than cells from rodents or carnivores.

The second paper, published today in *Cell* by a team led by Jonathan Ball at the United Kingdom's University of Nottingham and Etienne Simon-Loriere of the Pasteur Institute in Paris, independently arrived at a similar conclusion. The team analyzed its own 1610 sequences from the epidemic and also found that they separated into two lineages based on the single mutation in the glycoprotein. The researchers also compared pseudotyped Ebola viruses that matched the ancestor with ones with the same mutation, and **found they preferentially infected cells from humans as opposed to the fruit bat species *Hypsignathus monstrosus*.** They also found this mutant's infectivity was increased by other mutations, which suggests that the virus didn't undergo just one, but several adaptations allowing it to jump more easily from human to human. That could have complicated attempts to bring the epidemic to an end.

But Ball, Simon-Loriere, and colleagues approach this conclusion most cautiously, stressing that epidemiologic factors, such as "increased circulation in urban areas that in turn led to larger chains of transmission," likely were the most important driver. "Despite the experimental data provided here, it is impossible to clearly establish whether the adaptive mutations observed were in part responsible for the extended duration of the 2013–16 epidemic," they write in their paper.

A study published by *Science* in March of last year **did not find any evidence that the virus evolved to become more transmissible or more virulent**. But the first author of that paper, virologist Thomas Hoenen of the Friedrich Loeffler Institute in Riems, Germany, says the two new papers make a powerful case that the glycoprotein mutation benefited the virus. "The question now is, what does this really mean in terms of biological consequences?"

Luban stresses that Hoenen's analysis and others that reached similar conclusions weren't wrong. But the researchers were analyzing viral sequences to address different questions—such as the viral mutation rate—or only looked at samples isolated in the early days of the outbreak. "You have to do wet experiments sometimes," Luban says. "All of the algorithm crunching suggested Ebola is Ebola is Ebola. These two experiments say it doesn't matter what the computers say. The virus is more infectious."

The authors of the new studies agree that to clarify the impact the mutation has on transmissibility and virulence, scientists must do experiments with the real virus and engineered mutants of it, both in cell cultures and animals. But they have had difficulty finding a BSL-4 lab that's willing to collaborate and funding is a challenge, too. "We need to pay attention to this," Sabeti says. The rapid adaptation to humans underscores the need to respond quickly to animal to human transmissions of Ebola and other viruses, she adds. "Anytime you see one of these sparks ignite it could turn into full on forest fire."

⊘ **Assignment**: Have students revise the paragraphs in Example 3.9 to include topic sentences. Also have them insert headings to improve accessibility and shorten sentences that need revision to improve readability.

Example 3.10:
The Lancet Global Health, Volume 5, Issue 1, January 2017, Page e1

Precision Global Health: Beyond Prevention and Control

◆ The Lancet Global Health
  – David Taylor-Robinson, Paul Garner
  – **Campbell replication confirms little or no effect of community deworming**
  – *The Lancet Global Health, Volume 5, Issue 1, January 2017, Pages e2-e3*
  – Jason R Andrews, Isaac I Bogoch, Jürg Utzinger
  – **The benefits of mass deworming on health outcomes: new evidence synthesis, the debate persists**
  – *The Lancet Global Health, Volume 5, Issue 1, January 2017, Pages e4-e5*
  – Vivian A Welch, Elizabeth Ghogomu, Alomgir Hossain, Shally Awasthi, Zulfiqar A Bhutta, Chisa Cumberbatch, Robert Fletcher, Jessie McGowan, Shari Krishnaratne, Elizabeth Kristjansson, Salim Sohani, Shalini Suresh, Peter Tugwell, Howard White, George A Wells
  – *The Lancet Global Health, Volume 5, Issue 1, January 2017, Pages e40-e50*
  – Laura C Steinhardt, Yvan St Jean, Daniel Impoinvil, Kimberly E Mace, Ryan Wiegand, Curtis S Huber, Jean Semé Fils Alexandre, Joseph Frederick, Emery Nkurunziza, Samuel Jean, Brian Wheeler, Ellen Dotson, Laurence Slutsker, S Patrick Kachur, John W Barnwell, Jean Frantz Lemoine, Michelle A Chang
  – **Effectiveness of insecticide-treated bednets in malaria prevention in Haiti: a case-control study**
  – *The Lancet Global Health, Volume 5, Issue 1, January 2017, Pages e96-e103*

As we step into 2017 and look back at the past year, Zika undoubtedly stands out. 2016 saw the rise and fall of the epidemic in the Americas and worldwide spread of cases, until WHO declared on Nov 18 that the virus and associated consequences no longer constituted a Public Health Emergency of International Concern, but represented a "significant enduring public health challenge requiring intense action". As such, Zika joined other "enduring public health challenges" to which "intense action" has been directed for a long time, particularly other communicable and vector-borne diseases, on the list of health priorities. With Zika we are almost in uncharted territory: the heterogeneity in the natural history of the disease and transmission pathways still blur the picture of what is likely to be a long-term global health issue. Yet with some other diseases, a wealth of knowledge and seemingly defined course of action have not enabled us to close the chapter.

Much has been achieved on malaria, for example, but progress is fragile and we are still scrambling in areas where the burden persists despite decades of interventions. One major concern is resistance to pyrethroids used in long-lasting insecticidal nets (LLIN), a cornerstone of malaria control. During the 65th American Society for Tropical Medicine and Hygiene (ASTMH) meeting in Atlanta in November, *WHO released the results of a study* that shows that LLINs provide protection against malaria even in areas with resistance. However, in this issue of *The Lancet Global Health*, Laura Steinhardt and colleagues report contrasting results of a case control *study* in Haiti that raises doubts on the usefulness of nets in a low transmission setting, hinting that their mass distribution is not a panacea everywhere. In fact, a session at ASTMH explored key knowledge gaps in malaria interventions and raised thought-provoking questions on what is needed to finally get rid of the disease, given issues of resistance, uncertainties about newer strategies such as seasonal malaria chemoprevention or intermittent preventive treatment for pregnant women, and potential impact of the RTS,S vaccine. As highlighted during the session, there is no silver bullet, and success may only be found by putting multiple axes of pressure on the vector through combinations of interventions. The trick is figuring out what combination works in what setting, and that seems to be the next big question around malaria elimination: how do we develop decision tools to tailor interventions to a set of biological and social determinants—in other words, how do we move on to a more customised approach, through what could be called "precision global health"?

The idea of a "precision" approach to global health is not limited to malaria. Prevention strategies against soil-transmitted helminths (STH) for example have included water, sanitation, and hygiene interventions and mass drug administration, another imperfect and controversial intervention as highlighted in an Article by Vivian Welch and colleagues and two Comments in this issue. In their network meta-analysis, Welch and colleagues found little to no effect of mass deworming on children's growth, cognition, and school attendance. Eliminating the last pockets of STH incidence and prevalence will therefore require another precision approach, maybe one that combines controlling the parasites with working on more distal determinants of infection such as poverty.

A tailored approach will also help in reaching broader global health targets. The decrease in child mortality during the Millennium Development Goals era has been real but insufficient, and unequal. In some areas progress could be accelerated with more refined targeting of causes of death. Knowing where to target interventions to reduce mortality, by analysing the variability in the distribution of health outcomes for different causes would optimise efforts to reduce child mortality. A *study by Marshall Burke and colleagues* published in the last issue provides such valuable input, by identifying subnational mortality hotspots across sub-Saharan Africa in which the mortality decline is not on target to reach the Sustainable Development Goals (SDG) by 2030, as well as potential drivers for the difference in mortality. Spatial analyses of this kind provide crucial granular information—in line with a precision approach to global health—that could contribute to the progress towards the SDGs.

So beyond the essential steps of event surveillance and case management, on which the prevention and control of diseases are based, if we are to truly advance health and eliminate diseases, a case can be made for a tailored approach and the advent of precision-style global health.

Science Letters

This next science letter, in Example 3.11, pursues a different topic. It provides general readers with information about evolution, a familiar topic for students. Science letters can offer a large amount of information and can become fairly easy to write. Just have students follow the rules of good writing—topic sentences, subject-verb structure, clear language, and efforts to make the topic interesting. Here, as in the next science letter in Example 3.12, "Sunshine on a Cloudy Day," the author uses the photo for the same purpose.

Example 3.11:

Rethinking Migration

1. Charles G. Willis [1],[2],*,
2. Charles C. Davis [2],*

Author Affiliations

1. [1]Harvard University Center for the Environment, Harvard University, Cambridge, MA 02138, USA.

   Department of Organismic and Evolutionary Biology and Harvard University Herbaria, Harvard University, Cambridge, MA 02138, USA.

   May 15, 2015, Science magazine.org, Vol 348, p. 766

Letters

We applaud the Report by C. Montes *et al.* ("Middle Miocene closure of the Central American Seaway," 10 April, p. 226), whose geochemical analysis pushes back the timeframe of the shoaling of the Isthmus of Panama by 10 to 12 million years. This finding establishes a middle Miocene [13 to 15 million years ago (Ma)] completion of the land bridge between North and South America, marking a substantial shift in our understanding of the merger between these long-isolated landmasses. This has key implications for understanding the mass migration of organisms between these two continents—the so-called Great American Biotic Interchange (GABI).

Titanis Terror bird

Titanis Terror Bird

In light of this new hypothesis, previous inferences about the GABI require a fresh reassessment. For example, although the majority of animal migrations appear to have taken place during the previous estimate of when the land bridge was thought to have been completed (~3.5 Ma), the new date better conforms with evidence of older migrations (10 to 5 Ma) involving flightless animals such as ground sloths, procyonids, gomphotheres, tapirs, peccaries, and flightless terror birds without invoking complicated island-hopping scenarios (1–3). For plants, however, the route of migration across the Isthmus region appears to have been used much earlier. In the Barbados cherries, for example, numerous independent migration events from South America to Mexico occurred as early as the middle Eocene (46 Ma) based on phylogenetic inference, but increased six-fold beginning in the lower Miocene (23 Ma), just before the newly estimated date (4). Thus, rates of plant migrations between North and South America appear to have been greatly stimulated by the formation of this land bridge, even before its completion.

This reassessment raises a new conundrum: Why does the migration of animals lag so dramatically behind that of plants? It could be that even if the habitat was suitable, there were geological impediments to reaching it (dispersal limitation). However, the migration of flying birds, which conceivably could have overcome such impediments, appears to be as delayed as that of other animals, relative to plants (5). Another possibility is sampling bias in the fossil record. Alternatively, these patterns may hint at ecological, as opposed to geological, barriers underlying biome assembly. Ecological barriers could have included Plio-Pleistocene global climate, as Montes *et al.* suggest, or the need for vegetative changes to establish suitable habitat before the arrival of the animals. To the extent that this scenario applies, it indicates that geological barriers are not the only factor influencing migration at geological time scales and opens exciting new possibilities for exploring the relative importance of ecological factors in the merger of two continental bodies.

☑ **Assignment**: Review Chapter 2's notes on sentence length and keeping subjects and verbs close together. In *Rethinking Migration*, ask your students to analyze the topic sentences, sentence length, subject-verb proximity, and verb-to-word ratios. How do these techniques add to the clarity of writing?

Example 3.12:
Note in "Sunshine on a Cloudy Day" that the author uses a one-sentence abstract to give the reader the essence of the article. As we will show in later articles, abstracts, defined as specific summaries of articles and reports, work with the title to give the reader an overview of the article.

Sunshine on a Cloudy Day
David Schoonmaker, *American Scientist*, May/June 2006, Vol. 94 Issue 3. p. 317.

Clouds Sometimes Increase, Rather Than Reduce, Levels of Ultraviolet Radiation
At one time or another, most of us have proved empirically, and painfully, the old mother's tale that it's possible to get sunburned on a cloudy day. On average, clouds do reduce the amount of ultraviolet A and B radiation that reaches the Earth's surface and our skin, but it far from stops the damaging rays. Indeed, clouds are generally better at blocking visible light than UV.

Unfortunately, the average can, in some cases, be a pretty bad deal. Investigators have known since 1964 that clouds can have paradoxical effects on incident UV radiation. In more than a dozen studies since then, every data set includes at least some examples of what is known as cloud enhancement of UV. For people hoping to avoid skin photoaging and cancer, this can be a confounding characteristic. How much increase in radiation? It depends how you look at it.

Although the mechanisms aren't yet entirely clear, the degree of enhancement can be significant. Forrest Mires III with the Sun Photometer Atmospheric Network and John Frederick with the University of Chicago reported in a 1994 Nature article measurements of UVB at the Mauna Loa Observatory as much as 29.8% above modeled clear-sky levels. In various other studies, the range has been reported as a few percent up to 50%. Some of the most prolific authors on the subject are Jeff Sabburg and Alfio Parisi at the University of Southern Queensland and Michael Kimlin at the Queensland University of Technology. According to Sabburg, "In our latest research [soon to appear in the Journal of Atmospheric Research], we use new equipment and refine our methodology, and the highest UVI [an index of skin reddening] enhancement we found was 25 percent."

But those values are with respect to expected clear-sky UV. Compared with the level of attenuation usually seen when clouds are present, such measurements can actually be 50% to 75% higher than predicted, says Sabburg. And therein lies a conundrum for those who work or recreate out doors and depend on UV forecasts. No national forecast based on the World Health Organization's numerical scale for UV takes enhancement into account. Indeed, although several mention the possibility on their Web sites, the calculations instead assume that clouds reduce UV exposure. The U.S. National Weather Service and Environmental Protection Agency, for example, figure 89% transmission for scattered clouds, 73% transmission for broken clouds and 32% transmission for overcast conditions.

So how do we get more rather than less? Several studies suggest that reflection off the sides of cumulus clouds is one mechanism by which UV radiation can become focused. Sabburg and Joe Wong (then with the University of Southern Queensland) have also postulated that refraction and scattering of direct and diffuse radiation could result in markedly increased enhancement. Thus cloud conditions that include cirrus clouds thin enough not to completely obscure the solar disk, along with lower-altitude cumulus clouds, may lead to the perfect UV storm.

Just how common is cloud enhancement? The various studies have found that between 1.4% and 8% of all measurements show cloud enhancement compared with clear-sky values, depending on geographic location, but as many as 25% of those made on partly cloudy days may show it. Most often the enhancement lasts for 10 minutes or less—not a concern for the sun worshiper—but it has been known to persist for an hour.

The problem, of course, is predicting something that is influenced by systems as dynamic as clouds. A model was developed in 1974 that accounts reasonably well for observed results. The trouble is, just for starters one must know the fraction of the sky covered and the cloud optical depth—not characteristics that are predictable well in advance. As Sabburg says, "Our research is more aimed at measured, rather than forecast, UVI, but I think it would be almost impossible to predict these cases."

He does think, however, that authorities should do more to educate the public on the subject. Asked whether he wears sunblock on cloudy days, he replied "Yes! Unless it is overcast and the sun is not producing shadows—that is, it is not visible in some form—and there is no chance of the sun shining through broken patches of the cloud cover, I am still very conscious of the effects of UV." Bottom line: On a perfectly clear day, that UV forecast is likely to be quite accurate. Add condensed water vapor to the atmospheric mixture, though, and the outlook can become, well, cloudy.

✓ **Assignment 1**: Have students write a science letter on a topic of your or their choosing. The letter should have a clear, descriptive title, perhaps a one-sentence abstract, and then several paragraphs used to develop the letter.

✓ **Assignment 2**: Have students compare the science letter in Example 3.12 with the one on rhesus monkeys in Example 3.13. What value does the photo offer a science letter? Do photos help readers remember the article?

Example 3.13:

Figure 3.4 Ebola Is Placing the World's Rhesus Monkeys in Danger

Source: Sciencemag.org, 28 October 2016, Vol 324 Issue 6311, 435

Save the world's primates in peril

IN HIS IN DEPTH News story "Chimpanzee sanctuaries open door to more research" (29 July, p. 433), D. Grimm argues that partnerships between sanctuaries and research centers could see laboratory chimpanzees become extinct. This conclusion might be optimistic, given that new demands for precision medicine and neuroscience projects may lead to greater use of some species of primates in biomedical research. Worse yet, continued investment in research animals exacerbates the situation of wild primates in peril.

More than 70,000 monkeys are used in experiments every year in the United States (*1*). The federal government plans to invest over $434 million in the BRAIN Initiative alone in 2017 (*2*). However, very little funding is set aside for primate conservation. The continuing imbalance in interest and funding will see more wild primates becoming extinct, although accurate data are hard to find. The population of wild rhesus monkeys (*Macaca mulatta*)—the most common experimental primates in China—declined from 254,000 in 1998 to 77,000 in 2008 (*3*).

In addition, we are concerned that Grimm's story might deflect attention away from the plight of endangered wild chimpanzees. In the past 30 years, the Ebola virus has killed nearly one-third of the world's chimpanzees and gorillas (*4*). According to the International Union for Conservation of Nature, almost 50% of the world's 634 species of primates are in danger of extinction because of increasing human population, urbanization, tree felling, illegal capture, and climate change (*5*).

Most nonhuman primate species are found in developing countries that lack adequate capital, management, and technology to protect their wild primates. By contrast, many developed countries that lack indigenous primates tend to prioritize the value of primates for biomedical research rather than their conservation. Developed and developing countries should work together to address this issue. For example, to combat the decline of chimpanzees in Asia, where approximately 71% of species face extinction (*6*), the International Primatological Society should contact the decision-making departments in relevant Asian countries and establish an "Asian primatology alliance" to sustain

The population of wild rhesus monkeys (*Macaca mulatta*), a species commonly used in research, is declining.

wild primate populations. Such long-term international collaborations could redress the imbalance in capital and technology and save endangered primate species.

**Bin Yang,[1,3] James R. Anderson,[3]
Peng Zhang,[4] Baoguo Li[1,2]**

[1]College of Life Sciences, Northwest University, Xi'an, 710069, China. [2]Shaanxi Key Laboratory for Animal Conservation, Shaanxi Institute of Zoology, Shaanxi Academy of Sciences, Xi'an, 710032, China. [3]Department of Psychology, Kyoto University Graduate School of Letters, Kyoto, 606-8501, Japan. [4]Martin Hall, School of Sociology and Anthropology, Sun Yat-Sen University, Guangzhou, 510275, China.

*Corresponding author. Email: baoguoli@nwu.edu.cn

REFERENCES

1. E. W. Lankau, P. V. Turner, R. J. Mullan, G. G. Galland, *J. Am. Assoc. Lab. Anim. Sci.* **53**, 278 (2014).
2. White House Office of Science and Technology Policy, "Obama Administration proposes over $434 million in funding for the BRAIN Initiative" (2016).
3. Beijing Science and Technology News, "Primate rapidly disappearing: Gibbons will become history" (2009); http://blog.cdstm.cn/?uid-288984-action-viewspace-itemid-6370 [in Chinese].
4. S. J. Ryan, P. D. Walsh, *PLOS ONE* **6**, e29030 (2011).
5. A. H. Harcourt, S. A. Parks, *Biol. Conserv.* **109**, 137 (2003).
6. A. Shah, "Nature and animal conservation," *Global Issues* (2014); www.globalissues.org/article/177/nature-and-animal-conservation.

10.1126/science.aak9638

Adapting Chinese cities to climate change

ON 15 SEPTEMBER, Typhoon Meranti—the strongest recorded tropical cyclone to date in 2016 (*1*)—made landfall over the city of Xiamen, China. The winds and floods caused 10.2 billion RMB (1.6 billion USD) in direct economic losses (*2*). The havoc wreaked by Meranti makes clear that

rapidly urbanizing coastal cities must prioritize adaptation to climate change.

The destruction and degradation of coastal ecosystems impair urban resilience to typhoon disasters, which will become more intense as the environment grows warmer (*3*). More than 90% of Xiamen's natural mangroves, and a large area of casuarina trees and mud flats, have been lost to coastal reclamation since the 1960s (*4*). As a result, the natural coastal ecosystem no longer provides the ecosystem service of an effective barrier to destructive winds and storm surges. This in turn has led to further loss: More than 0.65 million (about 90% of the total) street trees were uprooted during Meranti's landfall (*2*). The rapid urbanization has also led to increased impervious surfaces in built-up areas of Chinese cities (*5*), which has caused increased urban flooding and related economic losses.

Chinese cities excel at mobilizing people quickly [e.g., more than 47,000 people were evacuated shortly before Meranti's landfall (*2*)], and they have enhanced early-warning systems that are crucial to natural disaster preparedness. However, they have lagged behind cities in other countries in incorporating adaptations to climate change into city planning (*6*). As Meranti demonstrated, and the New Urban Agenda highlights, these changes are key to reducing urban vulnerability and building coastal resilience (*7*).

Urbanizing Chinese coastal cities should develop climate-smart marine and coastal spatial planning that is resilient to climate change and minimizes carbon emissions (*8*). In addition, China needs ecosystem-based marine functional zoning, which identifies the critical components and

Example 3.14:

Figure 3.5 Tackling Toxics

Source: Sciencemag.org, 11 March 2016. Vol 351, 117 with permission from the author

---

EDITORIAL

Tackling toxics

Most Americans believe that if a chemical is in their cosmetics, their coat, or their couch, someone is making sure it's safe for their health. In reality, little toxicity information or regulation is required for 80,000 industrial chemicals used in commerce in the United States. To address this, legislation to update the ineffective 1976 Toxic Substance Control Act (TSCA) is currently moving through Congress. The hope is that it will lead to improved regulation of chemicals, but the extent and timeliness of the reform are not certain. In the meantime, the widespread use of harmful chemicals continues to pose a threat to our health and environment.

In 1977, Bruce Ames and I published a report that a flame retardant in children's pajamas called "brominated Tris" was a mutagen and potential carcinogen. Three months later, it was banned from children's pajamas, only to be replaced by "chlorinated Tris." We determined that this too was a mutagen, and it was removed from pajamas. Such regrettable substitution of a harmful chemical with a less-studied cousin is like "a game of whack-a-mole," according to Donald Kennedy (former editor-in-chief of *Science* and former commissioner of the U.S. Food and Drug Administration).* Unfortunately, highly fluorinated chemicals are now getting the regrettable substitution treatment. These chemicals provide stain and water repellency in outdoor clothing, nonstick cookware, furniture, carpet, cosmetics, and food contact paper. However, they are highly mobile, have no known degradation pathways in the environment, and can persist indefinitely.

Perfluorooctanoic acid, commonly called C8, has an estimated half-life of 2.3 years or more in humans and is associated with cancer, elevated serum cholesterol levels, and other health problems. C8 was phased out of consumer products in the United States last year, a half-century after toxicologists first revealed its potential for harm. It was replaced with numerous perfluorohexanoic acid (C6) compounds that are more rapidly excreted by humans but also show extreme environ-

mental persistence. Are these replacements safe? There is limited research thus far on the toxicity of the C6 alternatives. However, they are increasing in the environment and in human blood, and they share the potential toxicity of their C8 relatives.

One solution to the regrettable substitution problem is to address entire families or classes containing toxic chemicals rather than tackling them one at a time. For example, the Green Science Policy Institute, an organization of scientists that promotes the responsible use of chemicals, has called for a 50% reduction over the next 5 years in the use of six families of chemicals in consumer products, whose studied members have been found to be harmful: highly fluorinated chemicals, antimicrobials, flame retardants, bisphenols and phthalates, organic solvents, and certain metals.† Before using such substances in products, we should ask "Do we need this chemical, given the potential for harm?"

The good news is that companies are starting to act: Kaiser Permanente, IKEA, Levi Strauss & Co., and Crate and Barrel are phasing out highly fluorinated and other chemical classes of concern from the products they buy, produce, and/or sell.

Scientists can contribute by evaluating health and environmental impacts across a chemical's life cycle and looking for safer alternatives. They can make policy recommendations and collaborate on consensus documents. In 2015, 230 scientists from 40 countries signed the Madrid Statement,‡ expressing concern regarding the persistence and toxicity of both the highly fluorinated C8 chemicals and the C6 alternatives. Scientists can catalyze dialogue and action among manufacturers, retailers, and large purchasers and have an immediate impact in reducing the use of harmful chemicals.

Such actions by the scientific community can, along with meaningful TSCA reform, improve the health of the population and the environment. Most important of all, it will make our planet healthier and safer for future generations.

– Arlene Blum

"Do we need this chemical, given the potential for harm?"

Arlene Blum is founder and executive director of the Green Science Policy Institute, Berkeley, CA. E-mail: arlene@GreenScience Policy.org

*D. Kennedy. Science 318, 1217 (2007). +http://greensciencepolicy.org/topics/six-classes/
†A. Blum et al. Environ. Health Perspect. 5, A108 (2015)

10.1126/science.aaf5468

Published by AAAS

4

Planning and Presenting Oral Presentations: Discover Ways to Grab, Inform, and Persuade an Audience

Helping Students Plan a Presentation

Questions for Students to Answer

Audience

- Who is my audience?
- What do I know about my audience—backgrounds, knowledge of the topic, roles (students, teachers, parents, public), relationships and attitudes toward me and my subject?

Purpose

- What is my purpose in giving this oral presentation?
- Given my audience's backgrounds, roles, and attitudes, how should I shape the purpose to make my presentation acceptable to my audience?

Context or Setting

- Where will I be speaking?
- How much time do I have?

Content or Information to Be Given

- What ideas do I want to include or not include?
- Based on the audience and the context, what difficulties do I need to anticipate in choosing the information I will present?

Graphics

◆ What kinds of visual aids will I need to enhance the ideas I will present? Where should I use visual aids in my presentation? See Figure 4.1, which provides a PowerPoint presentation of this chapter.

Figure 4.1

"Help! I have to give a PowerPoint Presentation"

Guidelines for a Successful Oral Presentation

Sue Neuen and Elizabeth Tebeaux

Know your Audience and your Purpose

- Know whom you are addressing.
- Know what the audience expects from you.
- Know your purpose and the amount of time you will have.
- Remember that your audience will determine what you say.
- Keep your presentation as concise as possible.

Plan Your Presentation

- Create a title that will grab the attention of your audience.
- Avoid excessive detail. Stick to important points.
- Remember: Listening is harder than reading.
- Avoid trying to cover too many topics.
- Watch the length of your presentation! Nearly everybody hates long speeches.

Use a 3-Part Structure

- **Introduction**--Tell the audience your topic, the points you will cover, and the reason your topic is important to them.
- **Body**--Discuss each point. Accentuate the importance of each point.
- **Conclusion**--Repeat the key ideas you want your audience to remember.

Repetition of ideas is critical!

Introduction

- Establish rapport with your audience and interest them in your topic.
- State the main purpose of your presentation.
- Explain the importance of your presentation as it relates to your audience.
- Outline the main parts of your presentation.

Main Section

- Limit your presentation to main issues.
- Announce each topic as you come to it.
- Use visual aids, like PowerPoint slides, to help listeners follow your explanation.
- Use illustrations to help listeners visualize your ideas.
- Keep your explanation simple. Don't over explain!

(*continued overleaf*)

Figure 4.1 Continued

Conclusion

- Restate the key points you want your audience to remember.
- Help listeners visualize your message and then remember your main points.
- At this point, you may want to entertain questions from the audience and give them a copy of your presentation for future reference.

Structure of the Presentation

- Throughout the presentation, accentuate your movement from one point to another.
  - Help the audience know when you have completed the introduction.
  - Help them know when you have completed one topic and are beginning another.
  - Help them follow your plan.

Delivery Techniques--1

- Be sure everyone can see you.
- Begin speaking with no visual aids. You want people to focus on YOU.
- Avoid notes. Use PowerPoint, or at least an outline. Speak from the outline. Use a laser pointer, but don't wave it.
- Watch people as you speak. You can tell if you are not "coming through."

Delivery Techniques--2

- Always use some kind of visual aid, unless your presentation is very short.
- Make all visuals readable and colorful.
- Do not place too much information on any single visual.
- Introduce each visual at the appropriate time in the presentation.

Delivery Techniques--3

- Keep your body erect.
- Keep your eyes on the noses of your audience.
- Don't be afraid to use your hands for gestures.
- Move your body deliberately at major transition points in your presentation.

Delivery Techniques--4

- Rehearse your presentation, but don't memorize it.
- **Trying to memorize your speech will likely cause you to forget what you are saying!**
- Save all handouts until the end of the presentation. You want the audience to listen to YOU, not read.

The Four Goals

- As a speaker, you want to be remembered as one who is
  - Knowledgeable
  - Prepared
  - Well-organized
  - and Honest.

In short. . .

- Plan,
- Organize,
- Prepare, and
- Practice, Practice, Practice.
- Be sure the handout of your presentation makes sense by itself.

Style

◆ What level of language do I need to use, based on my audience's background and prior knowledge of my subject?
◆ What approach will my audience expect from me?
◆ How formal should I be?

Designing Each Section

> The structure of an oral presentation is crucial for one main reason: Once a statement has been articulated, the audience cannot "rehear" what has been said.

Remind your students that when they read and don't understand a sentence or paragraph, they can stop and reread the passage as many times as necessary. However, there is no "instant replay" when giving an oral presentation.

Audiences generally do not enjoy long presentations. Listening is difficult, and audiences will tire even when a presentation is relevant and motivating. For that reason, you need to help your students look for ways to keep their message as concise as possible. Be careful students don't omit information their audience needs, but help them look for ways to eliminate non-essential material. Again, without carefully analyzing their audience—their attitude toward the subject, the background, knowledge of the topic, their perspective toward the presenter—it is difficult to decide either content or arrangement of information.

Choose an Interesting Title

To grab their listener's attention, students must develop a title that reflects the content or subject of their presentation but does so in an interesting way. The title of an oral presentation should prepare the audience for the content or information to be presented.

Developing a Presentation Around Three Main Divisions

Helping an audience follow their message requires that students build into their structure a certain amount of redundancy. That means that they need to repeat or revisit main points.

> In the **introduction**, you "tell them what you are going to tell them"; in the **main body,** you "tell them"; and in the **conclusion**, you "tell them what you told them."

This kind of deliberate repetition helps an audience follow and remember the main points being made. (Readers can "reread" text, but listeners cannot "re-hear" oral remarks.) To design their presentation with planned repetition, students must clearly know their purpose and what they want the audience to know.

Plan the Introduction Carefully

During the introduction, you focus your audience's attention on your topic and the way you plan to present the topic ideas. Unless the introduction is effective and interests the audience, you will have difficulty keeping your audience's attention. An effective introduction tells your audience how to listen, what to expect, and the path you will follow in presenting your message. You may also wish to introduce your topic with an attention-getting device: a startling fact, a relevant story, a question, or a statement designed to grab your audience's attention and interest. Again, the device you choose will depend on the audience, the occasion, the purpose of the presentation.

Design the Body

In the introduction, have your students state the main issues or topics they plan to present. In designing the body of the presentation, they need to develop what they want to say about each of these main points or ideas. They may want to present their ideas in chronological order, logical steps, or a simple topical sequence. These methods will help the audience follow your students' ideas whether they are giving an informative speech, an inquiring speech, or a persuasive speech. The important point, is that a good presenter announces each point in the body as they come to it so that the audience knows when they have completed one point and started another.

Design the Conclusion

A strong conclusion should reinforce the points students want their listeners to remember. How they design the conclusion will depend on their initial purpose.

Choose an Effective Delivery Style

> Students should avoid speaking in a "written" style.

Encourage students to use phrases and to use a variety of sentence lengths. They should avoid excessively long, complex sentences, as listeners may have difficulty following their ideas. In general, tell them to keep their sentences short. They should speak as if they were talking to their audience or have them visualize the audience as one person. If students concentrate on getting their point across by having a conversation with the audience, they will likely use a natural, conversational style. Many suggestions for clarity in writing also apply to clarity in speaking.

Checklist for Clarity

- ◆ Avoid long, cumbersome sentences. Long sentences can be as hard to hear as they are to read.
- ◆ Avoid overuse of abstract or hard-to-visualize, many-syllable words. Instead, use concrete language that the audience can visualize or picture in their minds.
- ◆ Avoid overuse of slang and acronyms, unless you are sure that your audience will be readily familiar with such specialized terms.
- ◆ Use sentences that follow natural speech patterns, keeping the actor close to the action word.
- ◆ Use short, active voice sentences.

Use Techniques to Enhance Audience Comprehension

Because an audience cannot "rehear" ideas, once they have been stated, help students look for ways to assist their audience to follow their ideas:

1. Be sure students clearly state the beginning and end of each point and section of their presentation:
   - They should announce each main topic as they come to it. That way, the audience knows when they have completed one topic and are beginning the next one.
   - They should allow a slight pause to occur after they have completed their introduction, then announce the first topic.
   - After completing their final topic in the main body of their presentation, they should allow a slight pause before they begin the conclusion.
2. Remind students to always speak slowly, with energy, and enthusiasm. They should enunciate their words carefully, particularly if they are addressing a large group or using a microphone.
3. Help students use gestures to accentuate their points. A speaker should move his or her body deliberately to aid in announcing major transition points.

> Students should avoid standing like a statue in front of an audience.

4. It is important to maintain eye contact with the audience. Doing so helps students keep their listeners involved in what they are saying. If students look at the ceiling, the floor, or the corners of the room, their audience may sense a lack of self-confidence or uneasiness.

> Students should never read off the PowerPoint slides—doing this would cause them to turn their face away from the audience, losing eye contact and volume.

Lack of eye contact also tends to lessen credibility. In contrast, consistent eye contact enhances the importance of the message. By looking at the audience, a presenter can often sense the reactions to what is being said and make adjustments in the presentation, if necessary.

5. Do not encourage your students to memorize or write out their presentation. By doing so, their speech will sound as if they are reading it.
6. Have students rehearse their presentation until they are comfortable. Have them try walking around, speaking each section, and then speaking aloud the entire presentation. They should rephrase ideas that are difficult for them to say. Be sure they time their presentation so that it does not exceed the time limit.
   In giving a presentation . . . long does not equate with good.
7. If possible, have students record their speech. Help them listen to what they have said as objectively as possible. Remind them to consider the main issues of audience, purpose, their role, context, content, and style.
8. Coach their speaking voice. Are they speaking at a comfortable pitch for those listening? Is the way they project appropriate for your audience and their purpose? Are they speaking too loudly or not loud enough? Are they dropping the ends of sentences? Is each sentence easy to understand? Are they speaking too rapidly? Are the major divisions in their presentation easy to hear? Are any sentences difficult to understand?
9. Students should try *not* to provide the audience with handout material before they begin. To do so encourages the audience to read rather than listen. The audience can be told that the presentation will be available when they leave or can be sent electronically. If written material must be given out, be sure the material is coordinated with the presentation. That way, the presenter has a better chance of keeping the audience's attention on what is being said.

10. When your students are planning their presentation, help them determine how they will handle audience questions. They should prepare for questions the audience might ask and decide how they will answer each one. Again, unless they have analyzed their audience and the reason for their presentation, students will not be able to anticipate questions that will likely arise.

11. Keep the question and answer time moving. Students should answer each question as concisely as possible, then move to the next question. If they are faced with a difficult question, they should reword the question or break the question into several parts. Then answer each part. Encourage students to restate each question, for clarity of understanding and for any listeners who may not have heard the question.

Use Visuals Effectively

Examine Figure 4.1 again to see a PowerPoint presentation of issues to follow in planning a speech.

◆ Keep slides simple, as in Figure 4.2. Using PowerPoint helps avoid the trap of excessive data on slides. However, be careful: Power-Point allows almost unrestricted use of color and background.

Figure 4.2

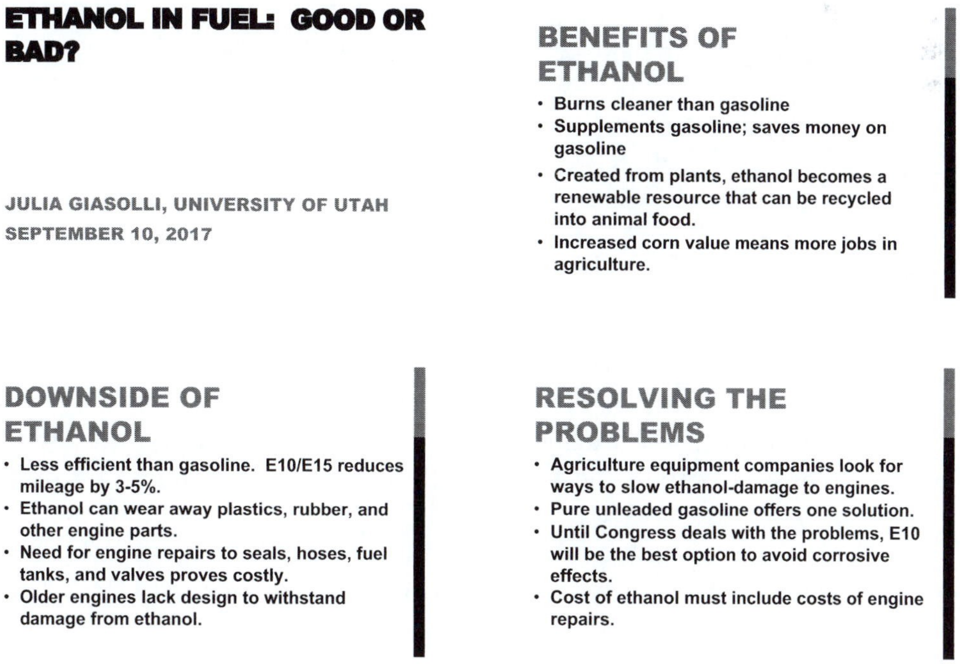

ETHANOL IN FUEL: GOOD OR BAD?

JULIA GIASOLLI, UNIVERSITY OF UTAH
SEPTEMBER 10, 2017

BENEFITS OF ETHANOL

· Burns cleaner than gasoline
· Supplements gasoline; saves money on gasoline
· Created from plants, ethanol becomes a renewable resource that can be recycled into animal food.
· Increased corn value means more jobs in agriculture.

DOWNSIDE OF ETHANOL

· Less efficient than gasoline. E10/E15 reduces mileage by 3-5%.
· Ethanol can wear away plastics, rubber, and other engine parts.
· Need for engine repairs to seals, hoses, fuel tanks, and valves proves costly.
· Older engines lack design to withstand damage from ethanol.

RESOLVING THE PROBLEMS

· Agriculture equipment companies look for ways to slow ethanol-damage to engines.
· Pure unleaded gasoline offers one solution.
· Until Congress deals with the problems, E10 will be the best option to avoid corrosive effects.
· Cost of ethanol must include costs of engine repairs.

Figure 4.3A

Figure 4.3B

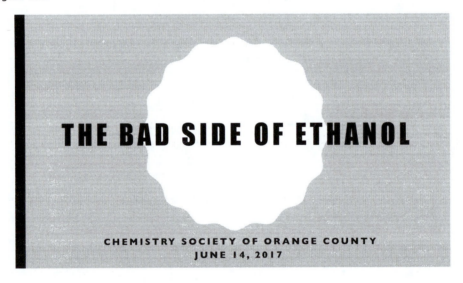

(It's easy to use too much color or a slide background that is entirely too busy.) Compare the opening title slide versions of Figures 4.3A and 4.3B, "The Bad Side of Ethanol." Which one do you think is best in conveying the title of the presentation? Color can enhance a visual, but it can also reduce the effectiveness of the message. Use good judgment in visual design. Students should use visual aids, but be careful not to overdo color or text. Encourage the use of easily readable fonts, large enough for the anticipated audience size and venue. It is often appropriate to use a picture slide to enhance a story—and it also aids retention.

◆ Students love to use animation. It helps to bring in and emphasize new points, keeping their audience with them rather than reading ahead on the slides.

> When using slides, tell the audience what they will see; show them the slide; give them time to digest what they are seeing; then comment on the slide.

◆ Students should not begin talking about another topic while a slide depicting a past topic is still showing. Few people can see, read, and listen at the same time.

◆ Always avoid using too many slides. What constitutes "too many" varies and depends on the context of the presentation. As a rule, students should use no more than 15 slides for a half-hour presentation. Practicing the presentation will help determine the number of slides.

Alternatives to PowerPoint

When your students become competent and confident in presenting using PowerPoint slides, encourage them to explore other programs and formats. Each comes with pros and cons, ease in embedding videos and documents, possibilities for adding animations and remote activation. Students will have fun exploring the advantages of the different formats to enhance their presentations. There are many formats to choose from, and we have listed a few with general descriptions below.

◆ **Bunkr** is a presentation tool that allows students to create presentations with any web or online content. They can easily embed content directly from many sources such as Flickr, Instagram, Vimeo, YouTube, Twitter, Tumblr, Evernote, Pinterest, and more.

◆ **Keynote** is an Apple Presentation Software for Mac. Updated for OS X El Capitan, Keynote provides easy-to-use tools that will let your students create and add tables, charts, shapes, photos, videos, and cinematic animations and transitions to their slides. They can work seamlessly between Mac and iOS devices and also with Microsoft PowerPoint.

- ◆ **PowToon** is a user-friendly animation tool. It makes it possible for your students to create animated explainer videos and animated presentations. An easy export system gets their PowToon animated video on YouTube or downloaded to their computer to do with as they wish. https://www.powtoon.com/blog/10-best-powerpoint-alternatives
- ◆ **Prezi** is a visual storytelling software alternative to traditional slide-based presentation formats. Prezi presentations feature a map-like, schematic overview that lets your students pan between topics at will, zoom in on desired details, and pull back to reveal context. This freedom of movement enables "conversational presenting," a new presentation style in which presentations follow the flow of dialogue, instead of vice-versa. https://blog.prezi.com/the-5-best-powerpoint-alternatives/
- ◆ **SlideDog** is software built specifically for your students who are presenting using "already made" presentation files. The idea is to use media files or a presentation program to create a playlist and then use SlideDog to present it to an audience. http://slidedog.com/blog/best-powerpoint-alternatives-presentation-tools-2015/
- ◆ **Sway** is a presentation software that makes it quick and easy for your students to create and share polished, interactive reports, presentations, personal stories, and more. Sway lets students include a video or add interactive charts. Sway's built-in design engine helps format their content and customize it to make it their own.
- ◆ **WPS Presentation** is, in interface terms, about as close to Microsoft's office software as can be found. Subtly ad-supported, WPS Presentation can perform just about every task your students would expect of a slideshow app. It's fully compatible with PPT and PPTX files and incredibly stable. The range of templates is impressive, and includes a stack of animations, transitions and effects for your students to choose from plus support for embedding Flash SWF files and most video formats. For more information see:

https://www.customshow.com/best-powerpoint-alternatives-presentation-programs/

Designing and Presenting the Written Paper

See Figure 4.4, a paper designed to be delivered aloud. Then read Figure 4.5, which is the same report prepared for silent reading.

Figure 4.4

Ethanol in Fuel: Benefits and Problems

Introduction

Good morning!

Mr. Bradshaw has asked me to explain to you, our local FFA, the benefits and problems of using gasoline that contains ethanol in engines of farm equipment. The abundance of corn and the increasing price of gasoline have made ethanol seem like the obvious solution to the energy crisis. However, when we look deeper into the issue, we find that ethanol has many flaws that possibly lower its value as a fuel alternative. Although ethanol does have benefits, the negative effects, from my perspective, over shadow the benefits.

Let's begin with the main facts about ethanol.

Ethanol at a Glance—The Main Facts

- Gasoline that contains ethanol is named from the percentage of ethanol in the mixture. (For example, E10 contains 10% ethanol and E15 contains 15% ethanol.)
- Congress has approved gasoline to contain up to 15% ethanol.
- Ethanol comes from fermented plants, such as corn and grain.
- Ethanol oxygenates gasoline, which causes the gasoline to combust cleaner and more completely.
- Those of you who live on farms which have corn as the main crop see ethanol as a financial windfall.

  But keep in mind that ethanol has two sides.

Benefits of Ethanol

First, ethanol burns cleaner than gasoline. As a result, ethanol, when added to gasoline reduces harmful exhaust emissions. Experts claim that greenhouse gases released by an ethanol-gasoline mixture are 12% to 19% less than pure gasoline. [1]

Second, ethanol supplements gasoline, which is often imported. Thus, ethanol advocates see it as a way to reduce dependence on foreign oil.   Ethanol, on average, is cheaper than its equivalent volume in gasoline.

Third, advocates see ethanol as a renewable resource, created from plants. Thus, many people see it as a solution to the energy crisis. [2] After ethanol is created, the remains of the corn are used for animal feed.   Ethanol can be recycled into the agriculture industry. [1]

Fourth, agriculture benefits from ethanol production because of the stability that the need for grains brings to the industry. Over the past few years, the price of corn has increased. This increase has a strong correlation to the increased use of ethanol in gasoline. The increase value of corn means more jobs and one way to improve the economy of America.

However, ethanol also has a down side:

Ethanol's Down Side

1. **Reduced Fuel Efficiency**

Yes, ethanol can be used as an alternative to gasoline. However, the efficiency of ethanol as compared to gasoline curbs fuel is lower. Studies have shown that E10 and E15 have produced 3-5% less mileage than the equivalent volume of pure gasoline. [3] This trend is magnified in vehicles with low fuel efficiency ratings. Recently, *Consumer Reports* tested a 2007 Chevy Tahoe with E85 and pure gasoline. The study showed a decrease from 14 mpg to 10 mpg, a 28.5% decrease, when E85 replaced gasoline. [2]

2. **Corrosive Properties of Ethanol**

Ethanol, an alcohol, is created through a distillation process. [4] Ethanol is considered a solvent, which means that it can wear away plastics, rubbers, and other materials. [2] This becomes a problem when the worn parts are inside an engine. These parts must be replaced regularly to keep the engine running at its full potential. Repairs can cost hundreds, even thousands of dollars. The residue from the dissolved parts builds up on filters and valves, and further reduces engine efficiency. [3] Seals, hoses, and even fuel tanks can weaken, causing interruptions in the fuel flow, and in worst-case scenarios, leaks of the highly flammable fuel. Older engines and parts are especially susceptible to the corrosive properties of ethanol because engine designers did not make these parts to withstand the damage ethanol could cause. [4]

3. **Tendency to Attract Water**

Alcohols have a tendency to attract and retain water, and ethanol is no exception. [3] When you store an ethanol-gasoline mix for long periods of time, the ethanol will attract all of the water in the tank. As a result, water will cause the mixture to separate. If the separated mixture is then used in the engine, the engine will not run properly and damage could occur.

Conclusion

The information provided should raise concerns about the use of ethanol in mechanized farm equipment. Although the increased use of corn, to distill ethanol, has provided growth and stability in the agriculture industry, the harmful effects of ethanol could outweigh its positive effects. While ethanol reduces the release of greenhouse gases into the air, the loss of fuel efficiency requires more fuel to be burned. The result: release of more greenhouse gases. This factor counteracts any positive effects the ethanol. You need to compare reduction of gasoline price with the cost of engine repair.

Agriculture equipment companies are looking at ways to slow damage of ethanol to engine parts. Using pure unleaded gas offers another solution, but until congressional action occurs, ag engineers must focus on making engine parts resistant to the corrosive effects of ethanol. E10 causes the lowest amount of damage, but many states have already shifted to E20, which has proven extremely corrosive.

One further point: the price of engine repair also has to be considered when you figure the cost of ethanol.

Questions?

Sources

1. Nebraska Ethanol Board
   http://www.ne-ethanol.org/facts/facts.htm
2. Highlands Today: "The Problem with Ethanol"
   http://www2.highlandstoday.com/news/highlands-news/2008/jun/22/problem-ethanol-ar-311037/
3. Bell Performance: "Bell Performance Fixes Ethanol and Gasoline Problems"
   http://www.bellperformance.com/fix-your-fuel-problems/ethanol-gasoline/
4. Energy Consumers Edge: "Problems with Ethanol Fuel"
   http://www.energy-consumers-edge.com/problems-with-ethanol-fuel.html

Figure 4.5

TO:	Jim Freeman
DATE:	September 18, 2012
FROM:	Christopher Joe
SUBJECT:	**Problems with Ethanol as Fuel**

Introduction

This report describes the benefits and dangers of using gasoline that contains ethanol in engines of farm equipment. The abundance of corn and the increasing price of gasoline have made ethanol seem like the obvious solution to the energy crisis. However, research shows ethanol to have many flaws that could possibly lower its value as a fuel alternative. Although ethanol might have many benefits, we can't overlook the negative effects that may even overshadow the benefits.

Ethanol at a Glance

- Gasoline that contains ethanol receives its name based on the percentage of ethanol in the mixture (i.e. E10 contains 10% ethanol and E15 contains 15% ethanol).
- Congress has approved gasoline that contains up to 15% ethanol.
- Fermented plants, such as corn and grain, produce ethanol.
- Ethanol oxygenates gasoline, which causes the gasoline to combust cleaner and more completely.

Benefits of Ethanol

Ethanol burns cleaner than gasoline. Thus, ethanol added to gasoline reduces harmful emissions. Experts claim that greenhouse gases released by an ethanol-gasoline mixture produce 12% to 19% lower emissions. [1] Ethanol also supplements gasoline, often imported. Thus, ethanol offers a way to produce fuel domestically and reduce dependency on foreign oil. Ethanol, on average, considered a renewable resource may provide a solution to the energy crisis. [2] The remains of ethanol created from corn ends up in animal feed. This dual produce feature makes animal feed a co-product of ethanol production, which can be put back into the agriculture industry. [1] Agriculture benefits from ethanol production because of the stability that the need for grains brings to the industry. Over the past few years, the price of corn has increased as shown in Figure 2. This increase has a strong correlation to the increased use of ethanol in gasoline. The increased value of corn produces more job. Thus ethanol, from one perspective, can create more jobs because of the increased value of corn. Some economists argue that ethanol can improve the economy of America.

Figure 1- Price of Ethanol vs. Unleaded Gasoline

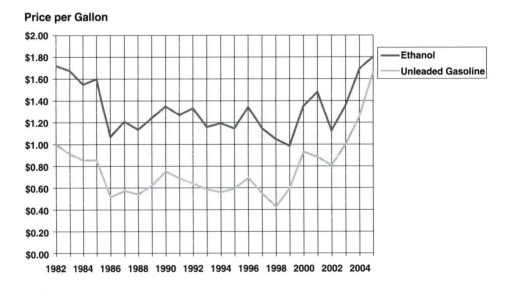

Image modified from source: http://www.theoildrum.com/story/2006/7/24/202222/351

Figure 2- Price of Corn from 2002 to 2012

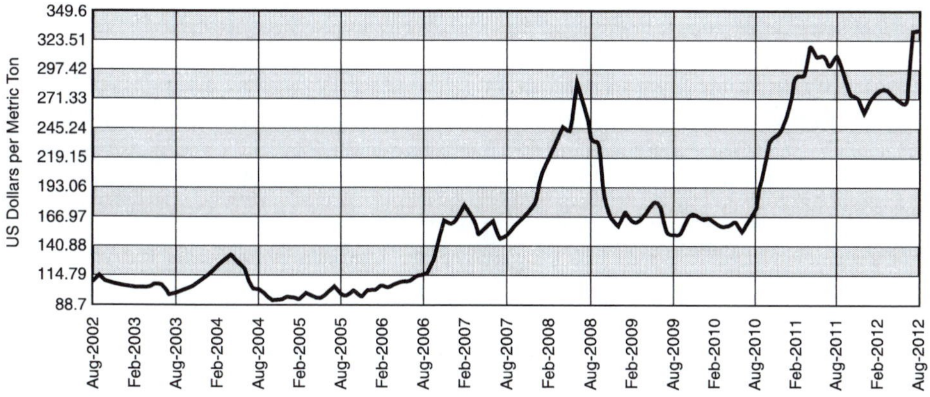

Image modified from source: http://www.indexmundi.com/commodities/?commodity=corn&months=120

Reduced Fuel Efficiency

Ethanol can provide an alternative to gasoline. However, many engineers question the efficiency of ethanol. Studies have shown that E10 and E15 have produced 3-5% less mileage than the equivalent volume of pure gasoline. [3] Engineers see this trend magnified in vehicles with low fuel efficiency ratings. Recently, *Consumer Reports* tested a 2007 Chevy Tahoe with E85 and pure gasoline. The study showed a decrease from 14 mpg to 10 mpg when gasoline was replaced with E85, a 28.5% decrease. [2]

Corrosive Properties of Ethanol

Ethanol, created through a distillation process, remains an alcohol. [4] Ethanol, considered a solvent, has a tendency to wear away plastics, rubbers, and other materials. [2] This characteristic becomes a problem when engineers examine the inside of an engine. Maintenance engineers must replace these parts regularly to keep the engine running at its full potential, and repairs can cost hundreds, even thousands of dollars. The residue from the dissolved parts builds up on filters and valves, and further reduces the efficiency of the engine. [3] Seals, hoses, and even fuel tanks can become weak, causing interruptions in the fuel flow, and in worst-case scenarios, leaks of the highly flammable fuel. Older engines and parts show major susceptibility to the corrosive properties of ethanol because they were not made to withstand the damage that ethanol could cause. [4]

Tendency to Attract Water

Alcohols have a tendency to attract and retain water, and ethanol shows no exception.[3] One of the problems with storing an ethanol-gasoline mix for long periods of time shows that ethanol will attract all water in tank. As a result, the water will cause the mixture to separate. If the separated mixture somehow ends up in the engine, the engine will not run properly and damage could occur.

Conclusion

The information provided should raise concerns about the use of ethanol in mechanized farm equipment. Although the increased use of corn to distill ethanol has provided growth and stability to the agriculture industry, the harmful effects of ethanol could outweigh its positive effects. While ethanol reduces the release of greenhouse gases into the air, the loss of fuel efficiency requires more fuel, which releases more greenhouse gases and counteracts any positive effects the ethanol created. Any reduction in the price of gasoline because of the added ethanol might seem significant, but when we factor in the cost of engine repairs as a result of ethanol, we find no cost effectiveness.

Our company, highly involved in not only the use of ethanol but also its production, should stay alert to its benefits and dangers. Concentrations of ethanol in fuel used for farm equipment continue to increase, and the company must take steps to protect itself and its products from damage. One possibility: get rid of the ethanol problem altogether by switching to pure, unleaded gasoline. The life of equipment would greatly increase, and this result would offset the slightly higher cost of fuel. The possibility of flooding the engine with water, due to separation in the fuel, would stop. Fuel efficiency would also increase with the use of pure gasoline and would increase the output of the machines. The company should also consider using engine parts more suited to resist the corrosive properties of ethanol. Currently, agriculture engineers perform a high volume of repairs on tractors and threshers because of the damage that ethanol causes to their engines. They could make these repairs much less frequently if parts withstood corrosion. While automotive engineers could work about the problems with the current amount of ethanol in gasoline, the amount of ethanol could soon increase to 20% or even higher. This company should prepare by addressing the ethanol problem now.

Sources

1. Nebraska Ethanol Board
    http://www.ne-ethanol.org/facts/facts.htm
2. Highlands Today: "The Problem with Ethanol"
    http://www2.highlandstoday.com/news/highlands-news/2008/jun/22/problem-ethanol-ar-311037/
3. Bell Performance: "Bell Performance Fixes Ethanol and Gasoline Problems"
    http://www.bellperformance.com/fix-your-fuel-problems/ethanol-gasoline/
4. Energy Consumers Edge: "Problems with Ethanol Fuel"
    http://www.energy-consumers-edge.com/problems-with-ethanol-fuel.html

Your students who are inexperienced in getting up in front of the class or speaking to an audience may be more comfortable reading from a prepared script or paper. When they have what they want to say in front of them on the lectern, they don't have to worry about losing their train of thought or forgetting important details.

Written presentations can be effective when a student plans and writes the presentation carefully and then utilizes a number of delivery techniques to enhance the effectiveness of the oral reading.

Structuring the Written Speech

The written speech has three main parts: the introduction, the main body, and the conclusion. Students will need to write each section completely. If they know that the speech will be published, they may wish to write it like an article for publication or a report and use headings and subheadings to reveal the content and organization of the speech.

Writing the Speech

1. After your students have designed the content of their papers and made final revisions of their ideas, they will need to give close attention to the sentences and paragraphs, since they will be reading these directly from the page.
2. Be sure that your students clearly separate each section of their presentations. Each section should have an overview that clearly announces that the new section is beginning. Each paragraph should also begin with a topic sentence that summarizes the content of the paragraph.
3. Check that students limit each section and each paragraph within sections to one idea. Watch length so that their audience will not lose track of the main idea they are presenting.
4. Avoid excessive detail, which often becomes hard to understand for people who lack expertise about their topic.
5. Students should use enumeration to help their audience follow their main points (first, second, third or 1, 2, 3) and clearly state when one point has ended and the next point is beginning.
6. Avoid long sentences. Long sentences are more difficult to hear and follow when they are read.
7. Help students clean up and polish every sentence to make it as clear and concise as possible.
8. Encourage your students to use an active voice whenever possible so that their sentences will preserve the natural quality of spoken language. They should use passive voice only when they want to hide *who* is doing what or *who* is responsible for specific actions.
9. Have your students type their presentation in a large type (12-point font or larger). Double or triple space and leave wide margins on each side of the page.

10. Have them place a "break" line or change the font color after the introduction, between each main point in the body (if the points are long), and before the conclusion.
11. It is best to underline, bold, or highlight important phrases or sentences throughout the presentation.
12. Encourage the use of visual aids, even though these may not be published separately. Again, use visual aids that will clarify any difficult or important points.

Tips for Students When Practicing the Written Presentation

1. Read each sentence aloud. Rewrite sentences that make you stumble or are difficult for you to say.
2. As you practice reading the presentation, try to look directly at your audience and speak important phrases or sentences directly to the audience.
3. Use overviews and topic sentences to announce each major topic as you come to it. To further alert your audience to the beginning of a new point, pause briefly; look at your audience; then read your overview statement or topic sentence. If possible, try to speak these to your audience.
4. As you practice reading your presentation, continue to listen for any sentences or words that are difficult to say. Revise sentences and paragraphs that do not sound organized, logical, and clear. If possible, replace difficult words with others that are easier to speak.
5. As you read, make sure you are heard, speak slowly, and enunciate clearly and distinctly.
6. Once you can read each sentence with ease without hurrying, time your presentation to be sure that it does not exceed a time limit if you have been given one. Set a time limit for yourself with your audience in mind.
7. Record your speech. Allow time between recording and listening so that you can gain some objectivity. As you listen, check for sentences that are hard to follow. Listen for breaks between major sections and major points.

Have your students examine the following report on childhood obesity. Note the use of the purpose statement that tells listeners what they will hear (Figure 4.6).

Figure 4.6

The Causes, Consequences, and Prevention of Childhood Obesity

Washington Junior High School PTO
November 12, 2017

Purpose

▸ To understand recent developments and research concerning childhood obesity

▸ To outline major causes of obesity in children

▸ To examine consequences of childhood obesity

▸ To identify effective prevention measures

Outline

▸ **Understanding Childhood Obesity**
  ▸ Defining Childhood Obesity
  ▸ Trends in recent years
▸ Causes
  ▸ Genetic and Environmental Factors
Consequences
  ▸ Health Concerns
  ▸ Economic Concerns
  ▸ Social Stigmatization
▸ **Prevention**
  ▸ Role of parents and schools

3

Defining Childhood Obesity

▸ Body Mass Index (BMI)
  ▸ Overweight- BMI in 85th – 95th percentile
  ▸ Obese- BMI > 95th percentile

▸ Defined differently in adults

▸ Controversial issues as children undergo rapid developmental changes

4

Prevalence in the United States

▸ Increasing rates of childhood obesity

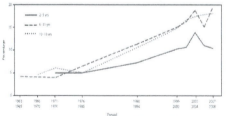

http://www.cdc.gov/mmwr/preview/mmwrhtml/mm6002a2.htm

5

Prevalence in Developing Nations

▸ Most overweight or obese children come from developing nations

▸ Attributed to shift in diet

▸ "Double burden of malnutrition"
  ▸ Infectious diseases and chronic conditions

6

Genetic Factors

▸ Strong correlation between parental and childhood obesity
▸ Genes associated with obesity:
  ▸ Fat mass and obesity associated (*FTO*) gene
  ▸ Melanocortin-4 receptor (*MC4R*) gene
▸ Influence growth and development at an early age
▸ Twin studies

7

Environmental Factors

▸ Prenatal and Postnatal Influences
  ▸ Maternal smoking, gestational diabetes and lack of sleep as infant
▸ Poor Nutrition
  ▸ Carbonated beverages.
  ▸ Fast-food consumption
▸ Lack of physical activity
▸ Lack of sleep
  ▸ Associated with high ghrelin levels and low leptin levels

8

Environmental Factors

▸ School Environment
  ▹ Promote junk food consumption
  ▹ Contracts with soda companies pay for school facilities
  ▹ Increases in portion sizes
▸ Television advertising
▸ Low socioeconomic status (SES)
  ▹ Fast food is a cheap alternative
  ▹ Less opportunity for physical activity
▸ Quality of home

9

Health Concerns

▸ Increased prevalence of chronic conditions among children
  ▹ Cardiovascular problems
  ▹ Type-2 diabetes mellitus
  ▹ Osteoarthritis
  ▹ Depression

10

Other Concerns

▹ Economic Concerns
  Obesity adds 9.1% to annual health care costs in U.S.
  Direct Costs: physician visits, medications, etc.
  Indirect Costs: morbidity and mortality costs
▹ Social Stigmatization
  Increased since 1961
  Study by Latner (slide 15)

11

Role of Parents in Prevention

▹ Mothers should maintain a healthy weight before and during pregnancy
▹ Children model eating behavior of parents
▹ Parents can limit the consumption of sodas and fruit juices
▹ Incorporate more milk, fruits, and vegetables into children's diet

12

Role of Schools in Prevention

▹ Nutrition education programs
▹ Restricting the sale of soft drinks
▹ Placing nutritional standards on foods sold in vending machines
▹ Promoting physical activity
  ▹ Sports
  ▹ P.E.
  ▹ Recess

13

Conclusions

▸ Developing nations have high rates of obesity.
▸ Increases in soda consumption and fast food intake have increased simultaneously with rates of childhood obesity.
▸ Conditions previously only associated with adults are now prevalent among children.
▸ Depression and obesity in adolescents are linked.
▸ Parents and schools can play the biggest role in preventing childhood obesity.

14

References

▹ Ogden, C., Carroll, M., Kit, B., Flegal, K. (2012) Prevalence of obesity and trends in body mass index among U.S.children and adolescents, 1999-2010. *J Am Med Assoc* **307**: 483-490.
▹ Food and Agriculture Association of the United Nations. (2006) Fighting hunger and obesity. <http://www.fao.org/Ag/magazine/0602sp1.htm>.
▹ Palca, J. (2007) Scientists identify a gene linked to obesity. http://www.npr.org/templates/story/story.php?storyId=9545915.
▹ Child obesity. (2012). *Harvard School of Public Health* <http://www.hsph.harvard.edu/obesity-prevention-source/obesity-trends/global-obesity-trends-in-children/index.html>.
▹ Latner, J., Stunkard, A. (2003) Getting worse: the stigmatization of obese children. *Obesity Research* **11**: 452-456.

15

Figure 4.7

Facebook in the Workplace

Help or Hindrance?

Mario Flores

Background

- Facebook exemplifies one of several social networking sites where users can interact with friends, family, and other employees through messaging, posts, pictures, and much more.
- Users can choose to have their profiles selectively or completely private.
- Users can also interact with fan pages made by companies or certain groups.
- How private is Facebook?

Does Facebook fit our Needs?

- Does Facebook provide a useful tool to review applicants and employees?
- Does the company follow the law when it retrieves information? [1]
- What should the company policy be inside and outside the workplace?
- Should the company have a Facebook page?

Part of the Community

- "If you can use social networking sites as ways to connect to real people... your business will do better."
- The company can respond to the public's complaints or concerns in real time.
- Having positive comments becomes a good way for customers to refer us to their friends.
- Do we have a big enough fan base to make a Facebook page? [3]

E-Professionalism

- Employees should also be aware of privacy settings.
  - Younger age groups have been shown to be more proactive in changing their privacy settings. [4]
- "Companies should adopt a social media policy to address use." [1]
  - "The safest legal path is to have a policy that clearly sets forth prohibited posts." [4]
- Problems with treating Facebook as a casual media site are similar to the early days of e-mails. [1]

Monitoring: Issues to Consider

- Legal repercussions may occur if discrimination occurs when Facebook becomes a tool for selecting/promoting employees.
- Some states have made it illegal to terminate an employee for "lawful, off-work conduct." [1]
- Policy evolves, and we need to stay up-to-update on it.
- The main concern of intellectual property being leaked might be a good enough reason to monitor employees. [1]

Conclusion

- We must take many issues into account when making these choices.
- Legally monitoring employees will help maintain the company's reputation.
- Meetings that go over company guidelines will be needed. [2]
- Without a public consumer base, the company doesn't need a Facebook page to receive customer feedback.

Other Points to Consider

- The default settings on Facebook don't include secure browsing.
- Why?
  - Facebook applications can't assure a secure network. [2]
  - Loading times are longer.
- If you aren't on a secure connection, your login information could be compromised.
- Is your company password the same as your Facebook password? [2]

Works Cited

1. Dryer, Randy L. "Advising Your Clients (and You!) in the New World of Social Media: What Every Lawyer Should Know about Twitter, Facebook, YouTube, & Wikis." *Utah Bar Journal* 23.3 (2010): 16-21. Web.

2. "How to Enable Secure Facebook Browsing." Quick Online Tips. N.p., 29 May 2011. Web. 06 Mar. 2013. <http://www.quickonlinetips.com/archives/2011/05/secure-facebook-browsing/>

3. Janusz, Ted. "Marketing on Social Networks: Twitter, MySpace and Facebook Demystified." *Key Words* 17.4 (2009): 124–125.   Web.

4. Osman, Ahmed, Andrew Wardle, and Richard Caesar. "Online Professionalism and Facebook: Falling through the Generation Gap." *Med Teach* 34.8 (2012): e549–e556. Web.

Figure 4.8

Best Approaches in Alternative Fuel Research

Prepared by Laura Bradt
Presented at Bradshaw Engineering Brown Bag Lunch

Why do we Care?

- Limited petroleum reserves will deplete and cost more

- Need alternative fuels
  - Can be healthier, cleaner
  - Need cost efficiency, scalability

- Bradshaw Engineering can contribute to this effort

Outline of Alternative Fuel Approaches

- Approach 1: Ethanol from Corn Grain
- Approach 2: Cellulosic Alcohol Fuels
- Approach 3: Soybean Biodiesel
- Approach 4: Biofuels from Algal Biomass
- Approach 5: Hydrogen (Ammonia) Fuel Cell
- Approach 6: Compressed Natural Gas

Approach 1: Ethanol from Corn Grain

- Ethanol and co-products can deliver 25% more energy than used in production

- Heavy use of agrichemicals
  - Nitrogen fertilizer releases N_2O
  - Eutrophication of waterways

- Use increases food prices; not economically viable

Approach 2: Cellulosic Alcohol Fuels

- Complicated process forms ethanol
  - Conversion of wood, grass, plant parts to sugar
  - Sugar fermented
  - Needs better catalysts
  - Higher pollution levels

- Feed widely available, not food crop

Approach 3: Soybean Biodiesel

- Soybean biodiesel and co-products can deliver 93% more energy than used in production

- Uses heavy agrichemicals, but less than corn ethanol

- Pollutes less than corn ethanol

- Food competition

Approach 4: Biofuels from Algal Biomass

- High energy density fuel from low energy cultivation
- No competition with food crops for farmland
- Water intensive
- More research needed to minimize competing algal strains and maximize biomass production

Approach 5: Hydrogen (Ammonia) Fuel Cell

- Uses chemical energy, Hydrogen very abundant
- No polluting emissions
- Batteries pose difficult disposal
- Use requires overhaul of infrastructure

Approach 6: Compressed Natural Gas

- Combustion engines need little modification
- Few harmful emissions, except NO_x
- Like hydrogen, demands new infrastructure

Conclusions

- Algal most promise
- Minimum Cost
  - Production less intensive
  - Grown on marginal farmland
  - Valuable byproducts offset high cost
- Maximum Scale
  - Can replace fifteen times more of nation's petroleum than soybean biodiesel
  - Low resource use
  - Lower emissions

References

- J. Hill, E. Nelson, D. Tilman, S. Polasky, D. Tiffany, Proceedings of the National Academy of Sciences 103 (2006) 11206-11210.
- B.D. Solomon, J.R. Barnes, K.E. Halvorsen, Biomass and Bioenergy 31 (2007) 416-425.
- P.T. Pienkos, A. Darzins, Biofuels, Bioproducts and Biorefining 3 (2009) 431-440.
- S.G. Chalk, J.F. Miller, Journal of Power Sources 159 (2006) 73-80.
- M.U. Aslam, H.H. Masjuki, M.A. Kalam, H. Abdesselam, T.M.I. Mahlia, M.A. Amalina, Fuel 85 717-724.

5

Communicating a Complex Issue: Examine the Impact of Major Science Articles, Abstracts, and Editorials

A number of major differences categorizes short science reports and major science articles. The major difference is length, which is often required to present a complex issue effectively and thoroughly. As we showed in Chapter 3, science letters, perspectives, and commentaries do not present their message with the complexity of a science article. If you study the examples in Chapter 3, you will see the differences when you compare those with the articles in this chapter. In addition, all articles should begin with a title that conveys the article theme or content and allows readers to know what to expect.

Abstracts: Informative and Descriptive

Long articles need to open with an abstract or a summary. Abstracts have two forms: informative or descriptive. The informative abstract contains the following segments: topic, a short justification statement, a statement of procedure used in the study, results of the study, conclusions, and perhaps recommendations. Example 5.1 exemplifies a well-defined informative abstract. It provides an effectively written synopsis that can be understood apart from the entire firsthand report.

We have identified the parts of the abstract to help you see them. Note that the abstract begins with the <u>project purpose</u>, then *focuses on the specifics of the methods used in the project*, and **concludes with the results**. Writers alert readers to the shift from procedure to results by using "**results**" as the subject of each sentence that announces the findings. Journals use key words, selected by the author, to create the index in which the article can be located.

Example 5.1: Informative Abstract

Chemical (Chlorpyrifos and Permethrin) Treatments Around Stacked Bales of Hay to Prevent Fire Ant Infestations

Key words: chlorpyrifos; permethrin, Lorsban 4E, Astro Insecticide, fire ants and hay bales

Abstract. <u>This research evaluated the efficacy of using a chemical barrier applied to the soil area under stacked bales of hay to prevent the red imported fire ant, Solenopsis invicta Buren (Hymenoptera: Formicidae), from infesting stacked hay. Specifically, we were interested in determining if we could protect "clean" hay bales stored in fire ant infested fields for up to several weeks.</u> *Chemicals selected as barrier treatments were Lorsban® 4E, active ingredient chlorpyrifos, which kills ants on contact, and Astro™ Insecticide, active ingredient the pyrethroid permethrin, which can also act as a repellent to ants. We established a series of 12ft × 12ft plots, with a 10ft buffer between plots along a fence row in a fire ant infested field. Plots were grouped into four blocks of three stacks each. Plots within blocks were randomly assigned to each treatment (four plots treated with Lorsban® 4E and four treated with Astro™ Insecticide, and four control plots). Treatments included spraying a 12ft × 12ft soil area with a 1-gal solution of each chemical and water formulation. After soil treatments, we placed four square-bales of hay, stacked two a side and interlocking in two layers, in the center of each plot. Stacked bales were sampled for fire ant infestation using 2.5 × 2.5cm olive oil—soaked index cards; one bait card was placed on each side of the top layer of hay in each stack.* **Results from ANOVA show a significant difference in mean infestation levels among treatments. Stacks of hay sitting in the chlorpyrifos plots had fewer ant infestations compared to the permethrin and control plots. Results after one week showed that only one stack in the permethrin, and two in the control plots were infested with ants, while none in the chlorpyrifos plots were infested. Results show that after three weeks all four control stacks, three stacks in the permethrin treatment, and two stacks in the chlorpyrifos plots were infested. These results indicate that on a short-term basis, such as 1 to 7 days, chlorpyrifos may be an effective short-term treatment option for protecting stacked hay from fire ant infestations**.

Ronald D. Weeks, Jr., Michael E. Heimer, and Bastiaan M. Drees, Chemical (Chlorpyrifos And Permethrin) Treatments Around Stacked Bales Of Hay To Prevent Fire Ant Infestations, Texas Imported Fire Ant Research & Management Project, Red Imported Fire Ant Management Applied Research And Demonstration Reports, 2000–2002, Texas Cooperative Extension Service. *http://fireant. tamu.edu/research/arr/year/00-02/2000-2002ResDemHbk.htm#stackedbales*

Abstracts differ from one journal to another. Be sure to have your students study the abstract—length, form, and style—to any journal to which they want to submit an article. Many abstracts have to be uploaded and will be limited to a certain number of words. Remind your students to check the number of words allowed before writing the abstract. They cannot upload more words than the abstract site will allow!

Descriptive abstracts begin with a topic and purpose statement. Then they explain the major segments of the report. Many reports have a descriptive abstract on the title page and an informative abstract on page 2. The descriptive abstract states what *topics* the full report contains. **Unlike the informative abstract, it cannot serve as a substitute for the report itself.** The descriptive abstract begins with the report purpose and then explains content areas or topics covered in the report. Note the difference between the informative abstract in Example 5.1 and sections of the descriptive abstract in Example 5.2.

Example 5.2: Descriptive Abstract

Multimodal Perception and Multicriterion Control of Nested Systems

I. Coordination of Postural Control and Vehicular Control
Keywords: motion, motion perception, perception, control, adaptive control

Abstract: <u>The purpose of this report is to identify the essential characteristics of goal-directed whole-body motion</u>. The report is organized into three major sections. **Section 2** reviews general themes from ecological psychology and control-systems engineering that are relevant to the perception and control of whole-body motion. These themes provide an organizational framework for analyzing the complex and interrelated phenomena that are the defining characteristics of whole-body motion. **Section 3** applies the organizational framework from the first section to the problem of perception and control of aircraft motion. This is a familiar problem in control-systems engineering and ecological psychology. **Section 4** examines an essential but generally neglected aspect of vehicular control: coordination of postural control and vehicular control. To facilitate presentation of this new idea, postural control and its coordination with vehicular control are analyzed in terms of conceptual categories that are familiar in the analysis of vehicular control.

Source: Gary E. Riccio* and P. Vernon McDonald**, **Multimodal Perception and Multicriterion Control of Nested Systems: I. Coordination of Postural Control and Vehicular Control**, *TP-1998–3703*, 1/1/1998, pp. 76, *Nascent Technologies, Ltd. **National Space Biomedical Research Institute. http://ston.jsc.nasa.gov/collections/TRS/_1998-abs.html

> ✅ **Assignment**: Project-based learning provides excellent opportunities for students to write informative abstracts across all disciplines. Assign your students to write an informative abstract about one of their projects. Ask them to use color coding or highlighting to identify the sections.

Summaries

Major articles may have a summary, as shown in Example 5.3. Busy readers need to be able to find what they need by finding the major segments of the article. Before your students begin writing their articles, each should select an example article from the journals to which they want to send their articles. Students need to look at the title, abstract or summary, introduction length, and article length. Then, they need to note the citation format used by the journal and the use and wording of headings and subheadings.

Example 5.3: Summary

The Global Economic Burden of Dengue: A Systematic Analysis

This summary comes from Donald S. Shepard et al. (*The Lancet Infectious Diseases*, Volume 16, Issue 8, 935–941).

Summary

Background
Denge is a serious global burden. Unreported and unrecognised apparent dengue virus infections make it difficult to estimate the true extent of dengue and current estimates of the incidence and costs of dengue have substantial uncertainty. Objective, systematic, comparable measures of dengue burden are needed to track health progress, assess the application and financing of emerging preventive and control strategies, and inform health policy. We estimated the global economic burden of dengue by country and super-region (groups of epidemiologically similar countries).

Methods
We used the latest dengue incidence estimates from the Institute for Health Metrics and Evaluation's Global Burden of Disease Study 2013 and several other data sources to assess the economic burden of symptomatic dengue cases in the 141 countries and territories with active dengue transmission. From the scientific literature and regressions, we estimated cases and costs by setting, including the non-medical setting, for all countries and territories.

Findings

Our global estimates suggest that in 2013 there were a total of 58.40 million symptomatic dengue virus infections (95% uncertainty interval [95% UI] 24 million–122 million), including 13,586 fatal cases (95% UI 4200–34,700), and that the total annual global cost of dengue illness was US$8.9 billion (95% UI 3.7 billion–19.7 billion). The global distribution of dengue cases is 18% admitted to hospital, 48% ambulatory, and 34% non-medical.

Interpretation

The global cost of dengue is substantial and, if control strategies could reduce dengue appreciably, billions of dollars could be saved globally. In estimating dengue costs by country and setting, this study contributes to the needs of policy makers, donors, developers, and researchers for economic assessments of dengue interventions, particularly with the licensure of the first dengue vaccine and promising developments in other technologies.

Funding

Sanofi Pasteur

A summary can be extremely long if the article itself is long. This summary is long enough to provide the reader with a sense of the material and findings the article states.

> ✓ **Assignment**: Students should know the differences between the two kinds of abstracts and a summary. As a class, discuss these differences and when each would be appropriate.

Articles

At the beginning of Chapter 3, we introduced you to One Health, its mission and purpose. In review, the One Health concept combines research in veterinary diseases and health with human medicine and research. We chose health issues for many of the articles in this chapter because we believe they are of interest to students, and they cover many disciplines. The first article, in Example 5.4, shares some of the attitude and information about the One Health concept. The short abstract in Example 5.5 provides a succinct rationale for this approach to human and animal medicine. Note the use of subheadings, a picture and graphs, references and notes.

Example 5.4: One Health, One Literature: Weaving Together Veterinary and Medical Research

Figure 5.1a

FOCUS

INNOVATION

One health, one literature: Weaving together veterinary and medical research

Mary M. Christopher*

Translating veterinary research to humans will require a "one literature" approach to break through species barriers in how we organize, retrieve, cite, and publish in biomedicine.

Translational research has begun to blur interdisciplinary boundaries, but a few, including those separating veterinary and medical research, persist. Veterinary medicine offers clinically relevant large animal models for a wide range of diseases and treatments in humans, from diabetes in cats to stem cell therapy in horses (1). Even as spontaneous animal models of human diseases merge into the mainstream of translational medicine, traditional boundaries in the biomedical literature—peer-reviewed journals and their knowledge domains—continue to reinforce separation between animal and human health by demarcating species-specific contexts for organizing, retrieving, citing, and publishing. To facilitate communication among scientists, physicians, and veterinarians, a paradigm of "one literature" can raise cross-species awareness and bring together new research communities and collaborations that advance translational medicine.

STUBBORN SILOS: "VETERINARY" VERSUS "MEDICAL" LITERATURE

What is the difference between medical literature and veterinary literature? The boundaries of individual "literatures" or discipline-specific journals are clearly defined in a bibliometric study or meta-analysis but are less clear in the context of a research or clinical study. Categorical silos—whether imposed by our own frame of reference or by an indexer—can impede the healthy and creative cross-exchange of knowledge, and at times such categories can seem arbitrary. Veterinarians might be surprised to learn, for example, that veterinary journals in Scopus include *Vaccine*, whose June 2015 issue contained research articles on human poliovirus, influenza, race/ethnicity, perinatal hepatitis, smallpox, childhood vaccination, and maternal im-

munity, with a single article on animals (Tasmanian devils). Physicians, in turn, might be surprised to learn that medical (but not veterinary) journals include *Comparative Clinical Pathology*, whose September 2014 issue included articles on dogs, rats, chickens, buffalo, sheep, goats, cattle, cockatoos, sturgeon, rabbits, and eastern hellbenders (giant salamanders), as well as the occasional human. Categorization of the veterinary and medical literature, therefore, imposes borders that do not always coincide with an intended focus.

"It is one thing to talk about the literature of a field. It is quite another to discuss

One Health. Human and veterinary biomedical research must forge a single path forward.

the literature used by researchers in that field" (2). Translational scientists seek relationships and pathways leading from basic and preclinical research—including research in animals—toward clinical applications. Publishing silos present a barrier to

this process and to new ways of thinking. Veterinarians often consult, cite, and publish in medical journals, in part because of their comparative training but also because medical research underpins many of the advances made in veterinary medicine (3). Physicians and medical researchers may be less familiar with veterinary journals and thus may not be aware, for example, that cats, like people, get chronic kidney disease and interstitial cystitis or that regeneration of mandibular bone in dogs using recombinant human bone morphogenetic protein 2 (rhBMP-2) was a stepping-stone in developing effective methods for reconstructing the human jaw.

Barbara Natterson-Horowitz, author of *Zoobiquity*, describes: "I, like most physicians, only interacted with veterinarians when my own animals got sick.... listening to the veterinarians [at the Los Angeles Zoo] on their rounds, [I began to see] that they were dealing with heart failure, and cancer, and behavioral disturbances, and infectious diseases, and really essentially the same diseases that I was taking care of in human patients" (4). Today's veterinary literature is replete with studies that inform our knowledge of human disease, and with fewer regulatory constraints, medical and surgical advances in animal patients can sometimes precede those in humans.

Failure to consider the broad literature can result in narrow context, omissions, and errors. An editorial about reporting guidelines in *Veterinary Record* cited *Journal of the American Medical Association* (JAMA) and *British Medical Journal* (BMJ) references to CONSORT but failed to cite REFLECT, reporting guidelines essential to the design of clinical trials in food animals (5). Cardiff *et al.* (6) described the failure of researchers to cite consensus reports, diagnostic criteria, and terminology published in part by veterinary pathologists for precancerous and cancerous lesions in mice. They documented numerous studies in which normal glands in mice were misdiagnosed as skin tumors, papillomas were misdiagnosed as normal epithelium, and runting was attributed to aberrant genes without excluding the much more likely (to a veterinarian) possibility of dental malocclusion. These misinterpretations have serious implications for the integrity of the multimillion dollar Knockout Mouse Phenotyping Program (http://commonfund.nih.gov/KOMP2), an NIH Common Fund project and part of the International Mouse Pheno-

Department of Pathology, Microbiology, and Immunology, School of Veterinary Medicine, University of California, Davis, CA 95616, USA
*E-mail: mmchristopher@ucdavis.edu

Figure 5.1b

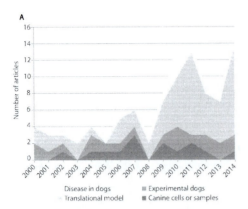

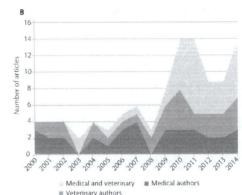

A
Disease in dogs ■ Experimental dogs
Translational model ■ Canine cells or samples

B
Medical and veterinary ■ Medical authors
Veterinary authors

Fig. 1. A meeting of minds. Physicians and veterinarians were collaborating and publishing together more than a decade ago. There has been sharp growth in translational articles and medical-veterinary collaborations involving canine lymphoma. Articles (*n* = 103) were retrieved on August 24, 2015, by a PubMed search on "canine lymphoma" (*n* = 930 from 2000 to 2014) filtered by "Human" species (*n* = 146) and excluding irrelevant articles (e.g., in which "canine" modified other terms). Each data point is the number of articles in 1 calendar year. (**A**) Articles relating to human lymphoma. Studies characterizing lymphoma in dogs compared the results to human disease, while studies of canine lymphoma as a translational model emphasized the application of the findings to human disease. (**B**) Articles sorted by author affiliations. Medical affiliations include basic science departments. Veterinary affiliations include both veterinary schools and private veterinary practices. Affiliation may not always match with professional degrees (e.g., veterinarians sometimes work in medical schools).

typing Consortium (www.mousephenotype.org). Journals contribute to such errors by drawing on narrow pools of peer reviewers whose expertise does not extend beyond the medical or molecular context to veterinary pathologists. But responsibility lies with potential reviewers as well; veterinarians may be reluctant to review manuscripts involving human disease, and both communities may be reticent to cross the imaginary line between animal and human work.

Failure to consult or cite literature across the medical-veterinary divide works in both directions. I have heard of veterinary clinical researchers, for example, balking at citing relevant experimental animal work from the "medical literature." John Young, veterinarian and director of comparative medicine at Cedars-Sinai Medical Center, has been a strong advocate of the interconnectness of medical research and veterinary practice, in part through public outreach for the nonprofit group Americans for Medical Progress. Translational efforts at his institution have contributed to the ability of veterinarians to use novel immunotherapies for treating glioblastoma in dogs, a model for human brain cancer, and brought together the expertise of a prominent neurosurgeon with that of a local veterinary internist, to use a high-definition

video-telescope for the surgical removal of pituitary tumors in dogs.

MEETING POINT: WHERE THE LITERATURE CONNECTS

Progress has been made in recognizing and strengthening connections between veterinary and medical literature. The World Association of Medical Editors (WAME) formally welcomed veterinary medical editors into the organization, thanks to the editor-in-chief of *Plastic and Reconstructive Surgery* and then-secretary of WAME. The decision recognized the parallel spheres of veterinary and medical editing, practice, and policy, including peer review, manuscript types, conflicts of interest, and reporting guidelines. Veterinary editors participated in roundtable discussions on biosecurity and dual-use research organized by the U.S. National Institutes of Health (NIH) Office of Biotechnology Activities. And since 2006, the Literature Selection and Review Committee of the National Library of Medicine has included a veterinarian on its team of physicians, nurses, dentists, basic scientists, and library and information specialists. Another important milestone was the decision by the British Veterinary Association to join with BMJ Group to publish its national journals

Veterinary Record and *In Practice*, based in part on synergies between physicians and veterinarians and following a successful joint issue on the links between human and animal health.

Importantly, physicians and veterinarians are collaborating on and publishing in translational research more than ever. Non-Hodgkin's lymphoma, for example, is one of the most common cancers affecting people and dogs; its diagnosis, molecular characterization, and treatment have been greatly enriched and advanced by comparative translational research. Based on a PubMed search of "canine lymphoma," filtered for "Species: Human," research articles involving spontaneous canine lymphoma as a translational model for human lymphoma have tripled since 2000 (Fig. 1A). Further, the number of papers authored jointly by medical and veterinary researchers grew from 0 to 1 per year in 2000 to as many as 9 in 2011 (Fig. 1B). Nearly one-half of the articles on canine lymphoma as a translational model were published in medical or basic sciences journals, but nearly one-quarter were published in veterinary journals.

These collaborations have also changed how the two communities communicate and unify biomedical languages. For instance, the term non-Hodgkin's lymphoma

Figure 5.1c

is not widely used in veterinary medicine (because Hodgkin's lymphoma is rare in animals, there is no need to make the distinction); but, as research on canine lymphoma as a translational model has increased, so too has use of the term non-Hodgkin's lymphoma (i.e., in the titles of articles in Fig. 1), from 3% in 2000–2008 to 12% in 2009–2014. It is clear there is strong impetus within the translational research community to "reach across the aisle" that separates veterinary and human medicine.

Translational research collaborations may explain the upward trend in cocitations between veterinary and medical journals in the Scopus database, which since 2005 have exceeded those between veterinary and agricultural journals for authors in the U.S. (7). This shift in alignment for veterinary medicine, from an agricultural to a medical focus, reflects the robust growth of companion animal specialties and evidence-based medicine and their accelerating translational applications to human health.

TOWARD A "ONE LITERATURE" PARADIGM

The One Health Initiative, endorsed by the American Medical Association and the American Veterinary Medical Association, embraces the concept that animal, human, and environmental health are inseparable and that the expertise of all health care professionals is essential for solving problems and advancing research (8). This premise lies at the core of translational medicine, where animal models of neoplasia, infection, and degenerative diseases inform medical research and where animals' relationships with humans extend to their role in mental health, cancer detection, war, sustainable agriculture, elder care, and domestic abuse. Translational scientists have begun to rediscover the value

of the uniquely comparative approach veterinarians bring to the biomedical table. The concept of "One Literature" extends the One Health approach to how we retrieve, cite, and publish biomedical research, removing contextual boundaries between veterinary and medical literature and facilitating knowledge exchange and collaborative approaches that benefit translational research.

To achieve this, One Literature challenges indexers to cross-list veterinary specialty journals under relevant medical specialties, focusing on similarities rather than differences. One Literature challenges editors to draw on both veterinary and medical experts in their reviewer pools to bring appropriate scientific expertise to the critical evaluation of manuscripts. One Literature also challenges publishers to develop collaborative veterinary-medicine ventures, such as joint publications, that facilitate connections between the professions.

Online innovations in scientific publishing, open access, and social networking already have opened new and exciting ways to transcend traditional disciplinary and journal boundaries and establish new relationships among articles (9). Open access enhances article visibility and retrieval and facilitates text mining, natural language processing, and semantic analysis, which add new value and functionality to traditional search algorithms, without regard to disciplinary silos. Just as social media have led to "context collapse"—bringing together individuals of different geographic, educational, and cultural backgrounds—so, too, digital publishing innovations are effectively deconstructing or "unbinding" the highly contextualized world of traditional biomedical journals and bringing together new research communities of scientists, authors, readers, and reviewers (10).

A future in which One Literature has displaced rigid notions of veterinary and medical research is a future in which translational medicine has fully capitalized on the essential connection between animal and human health.

REFERENCES AND NOTES

1. M. M. Christopher, A new decade of veterinary research: societal relevance, global collaboration, and translational medicine. *Front. Vet. Sci.* 10.3389/fvets.2015.00001 (2015).
2. E. Garfield, Veterinary journals: What they cite and vice versa. *J Citation Studies.* **5**, 464–472 (1982).
3. J. R. Page, H. K. Moberly, G. K. Youngen, B. J. Hamel, Exploring the veterinary literature: A bibliometric methodology for identifying interdisciplinary and collaborative publications. *Coll. Res. Libr.* **75**, 664–683 (2013).
4. C. Humphries, What human doctors can learn from vets. *Boston Globe* 24 June (2012).
5. L. Feetham, E. Raffan, Better research reporting for better patient care. *Vet. Rec.* **175**, 535–536 (2014).
6. R. D. Cardiff, J. M. Ward, S. W. Barthold, 'One medicine—one pathology': Are veterinary and human pathology prepared? *Lab. Invest.* **88**, 18–26 (2008).
7. M. M. Christopher, A. Marusic, Geographic trends in research output and citations in veterinary medicine: Insight into global research capacity, species specialization, and interdisciplinary relationships. *BMC Vet. Res.* **9**, 115–130 (2013).
8. E. P. J. Gibbs, The evolution of One Health: A decade of progress and challenges for the future. *Vet. Rec.* **174**, 85–91 (2014).
9. J. Kleinberg, Analysing the scientific literature in its online context. *Nature Web Focus* 29 April (2004).
10. J. Androutsopoulos, Languaging when contexts collapse: Audience design in social networking. *Discourse, Context and Media* **4–5**, 62–73 (2014).

Acknowledgments: I thank C. Hotz for insightful comments on an early draft of this article. **Competing interests:** M.M.C. coordinates the International Association of Veterinary Editors, which receives sponsorship from Wiley and Elsevier. She is currently the Field Chief Editor of *Frontiers in Veterinary Science.*

10.1126/scitranslmed.aab0215

Citation: M. M. Christopher, One health, one literature: Weaving together veterinary and medical research. *Sci. Transl. Med.* **7**, 303fs36 (2015).

> ✅ **Assignment 1**: Provide your students with the One Health mission statement (in Example 3.2), the "One Health, One Literature" article (in Example 5.4), and the "One Health: Science, Politics and Zoonotic Disease in Africa" article (in Example 5.9). Have students prepare a PowerPoint summary of One Health to present to parents attending a parent–teacher association meeting at your school. Students should follow the guidelines for a good oral presentation found in Chapter 4. Parents should come away from this presentation with a new perspective on medicine and understand that universities, particularly land grant universities, are merging human medicine with animal medicine.

> ✅ **Assignment 2**: Provide your students with the purpose of One Health found in the introduction to Chapter 3, the "One Health, One Literature" article (in Example 5.4), and the "One Health: Science, Politics and Zoonotic Disease in Africa" article (in Example 5.9). Challenge them to do some research on their own about One Health. Ask them to write a short persuasive article that highlights the need for One Health.

Example 5.5: Precision Global Health: Beyond Prevention and Control

This article is from *The Lancet Global Health* (Volume 5, Issue 1, e1).

As we step into 2017 and look back at the past year, Zika undoubtedly stands out. 2016 saw the rise and fall of the epidemic in the Americas and worldwide spread of cases, until WHO declared on Nov 18 that the virus and associated consequences no longer constituted a Public Health Emergency of International Concern, but represented a "significant enduring public health challenge requiring intense action". As such, Zika joined other "enduring public health challenges" to which "intense action" has been directed for a long time, particularly other communicable and vector-borne diseases, on the list of health priorities. With Zika we are almost in uncharted territory: the heterogeneity in the natural history of the disease and transmission pathways still blur the picture of what is likely to be a long-term global health issue. Yet with some other diseases, a wealth of knowledge and seemingly defined course of action have not enabled us to close the chapter.

Much has been achieved on malaria, for example, but progress is fragile and we are still scrambling in areas where the burden persists despite decades of interventions. One major concern is resistance to pyrethroids used in long-lasting insecticidal nets (LLIN), a cornerstone of malaria control. During the 65th American Society for Tropical Medicine and Hygiene (ASTMH) meeting in Atlanta in November, *WHO released the results of a study* that shows that LLINs provide protection against malaria even in areas with resistance. However, in this issue of *The Lancet Global Health*, Laura Steinhardt and colleagues report contrasting results of a case control *study* in Haiti that raises doubts on the usefulness of nets in a low transmission setting, hinting that their mass distribution is not a panacea everywhere. In fact, a session at ASTMH explored key knowledge gaps in malaria interventions and raised thought-provoking questions on what is needed to finally get rid of the disease, given issues of resistance, uncertainties about newer strategies such as seasonal malaria chemoprevention or intermittent preventive treatment for pregnant women, and potential impact of the RTS,S vaccine. As highlighted during the session, there is no silver bullet, and success may only be found by putting multiple axes of pressure on the vector through combinations of interventions. The trick is figuring out what combination works in what setting, and that seems to be the next big question around malaria elimination: how do we develop decision tools to tailor interventions to a set of biological and social determinants—in other words, how do we move on to a more customised approach, through what could be called "precision global health"?

The idea of a "precision" approach to global health is not limited to malaria. Prevention strategies against soil-transmitted helminths (STH) for example have included water, sanitation, and hygiene interventions and mass drug administration, another imperfect and controversial intervention as highlighted in an Article by Vivian Welch and colleagues and two Comments in this issue. In their network meta-analysis, Welch and colleagues found little to no effect of mass deworming on children's growth, cognition, and school attendance. Eliminating the last pockets of STH incidence and prevalence will therefore require another precision approach, maybe one that combines controlling the parasites with working on more distal determinants of infection such as poverty.

A tailored approach will also help in reaching broader global health targets. The decrease in child mortality during the Millennium Development Goals era has been real but insufficient, and unequal. In some areas progress could be accelerated with more refined targeting of causes of death. Knowing where to target interventions to reduce mortality, by analysing the variability in the distribution of health outcomes for different causes would optimise efforts to reduce child mortality. A *study by Marshall Burke and colleagues* published in the last issue provides such valuable input, by identifying subnational mortality hotspots across sub-Saharan Africa in which the mortality decline is not on target to reach the Sustainable Development Goals (SDG) by 2030, as well as potential drivers for the difference in mortality. Spatial analyses of this kind provide crucial granular information—in line with a precision approach to global health—that could contribute to the progress towards the SDGs.

So beyond the essential steps of event surveillance and case management, on which the prevention and control of diseases are based, if we are to truly advance health and eliminate diseases, a case can be made for a tailored approach and the advent of precision-style global health.

The National High School Journal of Science

As a teacher, you may be thinking "If my students did write good articles of substance, where could they be submitted for review and publication or posting?" One option is the *National High School Journal of Science*. The following paragraphs were taken from the National High School Journal of Science website (nhsjs.com):

> The *National High School Journal of Science* is a free, online, student-run and peer-reviewed research journal that is targeted towards high school students. Striving to bring science to a wider audience and engaging students in learning beyond the classroom walls, our journal hopes to expose young people to new ideas and topics. This high school student-run science journal always welcomes aspiring scientists to submit articles and to get involved with our publishing process.
>
> Though run by students, we maintain high standards for publication thanks to the work of our dedicated peer reviewers and experienced Scientist Advisory Board, consisting of professional researchers. Our publications fall under two main categories: original research done by high school students and articles describing significant developments in science and policy; other content includes interviews with experienced scientists and advice for aspiring researchers.
>
> At NHSJS, we're looking to restore the excitement of STEM, and to inspire the next generation of scientists. Science is about pushing into the unknown and questioning dogma, and in many ways, a student-run research journal represents those very ideals.

We encourage you to check out the website yourself and also share it with your students. As your students advance in *Writing Science Right*, they may want to look at the submission requirements and enter their research or writings for review and posting.

Examples 5.6 and 5.7 illustrate what high school students are capable of writing. Both were published on the *National High School Journal of Science* website.

Example 5.6: Nanotechnology and the New Age of Cancer Treatment

Charley Ren, Winter 2012 Issue, **NHSJS**
November 16, 2012

Many of you may be familiar with the standard chemotherapy and radiation therapy treatments used for cancer treatment. However, much of the research over the past decade has pointed to the arrival of a new approach to cancer treatment—the use of nanotechnology. Nanotechnology is a new branch of science that engineers on the atomic and molecular level utilize to create particles and structures with novel physical and chemical properties [1]. Although we often hear of nanotechnology being incorporated into systems like computers or even microscopes, this new technology may be our "magic bullet" for the world's longstanding cancer struggle. The new technology has much potential use in the diagnosis and treatment of cancer. Currently, nanotechnology in the field of cancer is working towards the development of nanoparticles or vectors that target cancerous cells with drugs and imaging agents, or nanosensors that can detect biological signs of cancer [1]. Nanosensors are particles engineered to target specific molecules and biological matter in order to detect and analyze matter on the nano-scale. For example, nanocrystals can be used to label certain cells and tissues by emitting light of a certain wavelength [2]. Recently in 2010, Yale scientists have developed the first nanosensor that can detect cancer in "whole blood" (in the actual human) without having to extract and purify blood from the human. The sensor can be used to detect breast cancer and prostate cancer in the bloodstream, in quantities low as several nanograms [3]. In the same year, a research team from the Israel Institute of Technology used nanosensors made of gold nanoparticles to differentiate between healthy patients and patients with lung, breast, prostate, or colorectal cancers through the analyzation of a single exhaled breath [4]. Thus, these promising new sensors may be utilized as detectors for various types of cancers in their early stages and in multiple body fluids—possibly improving the chances of full recovery through early diagnosis.

In addition to nanosensors, nanovectors, otherwise known as "nanoparticles," are being developed as delivery agents for both anti-cancer drugs and imaging agents. Standard treatments like ionizing radiation and sometimes even chemotherapy may affect normal tissues in addition to cancerous tumors. The reason? Scientists are constantly struggling to find effective means of delivering anti-cancer treatment (e.g. radiation or drugs) directly to specific tumor sites—slight miscalculations and imprecisions in the administration of these agents can easily affect the healthy neighboring tissues. Nanotechnology has the potential of overcoming these prior difficulties by crafting "nanoparticles" that have properties that allow them to specifically target cancer cells once absorbed into the body [1]. Most cancer-targeted nanoparticles are referred to as "Nanocarriers." While standard chemotherapy delivers anticancer agents or drugs through injection and pill, the development of nanocarriers may render standard chemotherapy moot [5]. Nanocarriers are nanoparticles that can carry and deliver anticancer drugs with high-specificity to cancer cells. Advantages over free drugs are numerous; if built well, nanocarriers can: protect drugs from degrading, protect drugs from interacting with non-cancerous environments, enhance absorption of drugs into tumors, and target specific cancer pathways within the body. Currently, typical nanocarriers are built from natural and synthetic polymers and lipid molecules. However, other nanocarriers include nanoshells built from gold and silica, gold nanoparticles, nanocages, and other materials [6]. Despite its promising future, most nanoparticles and sensors are still in development phase. Various cancers and even tumors are extremely heterogeneous in composition; thus each nanocarrier often has to be tailored specifically to the pharmacokinetics (bodily pathways) of a specific individual and specific tumors. As a result, one type of nanocarrier may not be universally potent for a wide patient population as its effectiveness varies from individual to individual. Thus, in-vivo (live) studies on actual patients are difficult because nanocarriers must be experimentally determined on a case-by-case basis [6]. As with most new and promising innovations in the medical field, wide-spread application may require a few more decades of further research and development. Nevertheless, although we are still far from a panacea, this coming decade holds much promise for the future of cancer nanotechnology.

1. "Learn About Nanotechnology in Cancer." (2012). *National Cancer Institute Alliance for Nanotechnology in Cancer.* http://nano.cancer.gov/learn/ (9/21/12).
2. "What Are Nanosensors and Why Are They Important in Medical Applications?" (2006). *University of Illinois at Chicago College of Engineering.* http://tigger.uic.edu/depts/nanotechcenter/wan.htm (9/21/12).
3. "Nanosensor Detects Cancer in Whole Blood." (2010). *Nanotechweb.org.* http://nanotechweb.org/cws/article/tech/41407 (9/21/12).
4. "Nanosensors Detect Signs of Cancer in Human Breath." (2010). *National Cancer Institute Alliance for Nanotechnology in Cancer.* http://nano.cancer.gov/action/news/2010/aug/nanotech_news_2010-08-17c.asp (9/21/12).
5. "Treating Cancer With Chemotherapy" (2011). *Chemotherapy.com.* www.chemotherapy.com/treating_with_chemo/treating_with_chemo.html (9/21/12).
6. Peer, D., J.M. Karp, S. Hong, O.C. Farokhzad, R. Margalit, R. Langer. 2007. Nanocarriers as an emerging platform for cancer therapy. *Nat. Nanotechnol.* **2**:751–760.

Example 5.7: West Nile Virus: From Mechanisms to Novel Research Techniques

Posted by: Jennifer Dong Tags: Posted date: August 7, 2016 | **NHSJS**

Abstract

The West Nile Virus was first introduced to the Unites States in the early 21st century. Along with the rise of this new virus, panic spread as well. However, with the development of many new serologic techniques and the even more recent real-time reverse transcription PCR technique, early and specific detection of this virus is now possible and will lead to fewer epidemics in the future.

Introduction

Outbreaks of the West Nile Virus (WNV) have been reemerging ever since its first documentation in 1937 from the West Nile District of Northern Uganda. From 1999 to 2003, the epidemic spread west across the North American continent. Following a slight drop in 2003, cases reappeared in 2005–2007 and 2012, with the most recent reports occurring in the summer of 2014 [1]. Because the West Nile Virus has become well established in North America, infesting a variety of hosts such as people, birds, and horses, it has become a *health* priority to develop rapid and accurate diagnostic techniques [2]. It is predicted that since this virus has spread so quickly in the past, it will likely to continue this pattern of dissemination in the future. Early detection can help *environmental* engineers and other scientists quarantine certain areas to prevent future epidemics [1].

Molecular Mechanisms and Pathogenesis

The WNV belongs to the *Flavivirus* genus and *Flaviridae* family. Other common pathogenic flaviviruses include Japanese encephalitis (JE), yellow fever (YF), and Murray Valley encephalitis (MVE) [1]. The spherical viral structure consists of a nucleocapsid surrounded by a lipid bilayer. The single-stranded RNA resides inside the nucleocapsid and is characterized by a positive polarity and an open reading frame (Shi, Pei Yong, and Susan J. Wong. "Serologic Diagnosis of West Nile Virus Infection." [2] Expert Review of Molecular Diagnostics, November 2003, 733–41. June 26, 2016). Flaviviruses need two factors to be maintained in nature: a vector and a host. Most commonly, mosquitoes act as the vector and wild avian *species* act as the host. Through a mosquito-avian transmission cycle, WNV is maintained and amplified [3].

Clinical Presentations

Symptoms of WNV vary across different species ranging from severe symptoms to asymptomatic. In birds, infection causes extreme viraemia and inflammation. Shortly afterwards, tissues, internal organs, and the central nervous system (CNS) suffer necrosis and hemorrhaging. Viraemia is lower in horses; however, clinical signs include CNS lesions, muscular fasciculation, and weakness. Humans typically show no symptoms; however, some will display West Nile Fever [4]. There are currently no treatments available for humans. Severe cases would require hospitalization in order to receive supportive *treatment*. Although these treatments can reduce pain and discomfort, they do not directly combat the virus.

MAC ELISA

In laboratory studies, MAC ELISAs (IgM *antibody* capture enzyme-linked immunosorbent assays) have started to become more widely used because of its many advantages. The technique is sensitive for early detection and avoids the influence of IgG antibodies. After the onset of WNV infection, IgM antibodies are released into the bloodstream. MAC ELISAs are used as an *indicator* of recent infection and function to detect IgM levels in the bloodstream. In the first step of a MAC ELISA, goat anti-IgM is used as capture antibodies. Blocking of the test plates with nonfat dry milk is important because it reduces nonspecific binding and background. Subsequently, human sera are added to the plate to react with the antihuman IgM, viral antigens are added to react with the serum antibodies, and labeled monoclonal antibody (mAb) is added to react with the antigens. Finally, the substrate tetra methyl benzidine is added. Using a microplate reader, the absorbance of the test serum is compared to the absorbance of the negative control sample. The respective ratio must be greater than 2.0 in order to be considered a positive result. However, many disadvantages also exist including the need for follow up testing and the possibility of cross-reactions with other similar flaviviruses such as JE or YF [4].

Fluorescent Microsphere Immunoassay

A relatively new technique, immunoassays are able to portray zones on nitrocellulose membranes by using microspheres with bound antigens and lateral flow immunochromatography *technology*. After incubation of human or horse samples, the antibodies bound to the microspheres can be detected with species-specific secondary antibodies. In comparison with ELISAs, microsphere immunoassays have several advantages. This technique, more quantitative, requires shorter time due to the shaking *motion* during incubation; and the analysis has higher precision, which calls for less valuable specimen volumes [5]. Purified WNV recombinant E, NS3, and NS5 proteins were tested with this method. We found the NS3 *protein* produced unreliable results from the test; however, the E and NS5 proteins demonstrated the capacity to be used as reliable diagnostic tools for humans in the future [1].

RT-qPCR

Reverse transcription quantitative polymerase chain reaction has become the most recent diagnostic technique. This technique transcribes the virus RNA into DNA with the enzyme reverse transcriptase. After producing the DNA template and the annealing of two primers, extension occurs. Through many subsequent cycles, the DNA is amplified to the desired amount [6]. The primer is sequence specific to the WNV RNA, so if amplification occurs the test is positive, but if amplification fails, the test is negative [7]. However, one disadvantage is that negative results do not guarantee that the serum is not infected with WNV [8].

Future Outlook

MAC ELISAs and microsphere immunoassays will continue to play an important role for human diagnostic tests. One advantage of the microsphere immunoassay is its ability to detect multiple antigens in a single test. A disadvantage is the inability to differentiate between the similar flaviviruses that have infected the same geographical location due to cross-reaction. One solution was the development of RT-qPCR, a nucleic-acid based assay that targets the RNA sequences of the WNV virus ("West Nile Virus: Detection with Serologic and Real-time PCR Assays." *Quest Diagnostics*. Quest Diagnostics, 2013. Web. 24 June 2016. "WNV Antibody Testing." Centers for *Disease* Control and Prevention. February 12, 2015. Accessed July 24, 2016.). However, negative results require follow up testing for confirmation. Therefore, new techniques should be developed that do not cross react to use along with RT-qPCR. Furthermore, currently no vaccine or cures exist against this virus for humans. The only successes in *research* have been in vaccine development for horses and only supportive care exists for humans. Therefore, a pressing current priority is to develop a WNV vaccine that is specific to humans.

Citations

1. Shi, Pei Yong, and Susan J. Wong. "Serologic Diagnosis of West Nile Virus Infection." Expert Review of Molecular Diagnostics, November 2003, 733–41. June 26, 2016.
2. Hirota Jiro, Shinya Shimizu, and Tomoyuki Shibahara. "Application of West Nile Virus Diagnostic Techniques." Expert Review of Anti-infective Therapy, August 2013, 4–22. June 26, 2016. http://dx.doi.org.libproxy.temple.edu/10.1586/147 87210.2013.814824

3. McVey, D. S., W. C. Wilson, and C. G. Gay. "West Nile Virus." Revue scientifique et technique (International Office of Epizootics), 2015, 431–39. June 26, 2016. Pubmed.

4. "West Nile Virus: Detection With Serologic and Real-time PCR Assays." *Quest Diagnostics.* Quest Diagnostics, 2013. Web. 24 June 2016. www.questdiagnostics. com/testcenter/testguide.action%3Fdc%3DCF_WestNileVirus

5. "WNV Antibody Testing." *Centers for Disease Control and Prevention.* February 12, 2015. Accessed July 24, 2016. www.cdc.gov/westnile/healthcareproviders/ healthcareproviders-diagnostic.html

6. White, Bruce A. *PCR Cloning Protocols.* Vol. 67. Totowa, NJ: Humana Press, 1997.

Be Sociable, Share!

1. Shi, Pei Yong, and Susan J. Wong. "Serologic Diagnosis of West Nile Virus Infection." Expert Review of Molecular Diagnostics, November 2003, 733–41. June 26, 2016.

2. McVey, D. S., W. C. Wilson, and C. G. Gay. "West Nile Virus." Revue scientifique et technique (International Office of Epizootics), 2015, 431–39. June 26, 2016. Pubmed.

3. Hirota Jiro, Shinya Shimizu, and Tomoyuki Shibahara. "Application of West Nile Virus Diagnostic Techniques."

4. Expert Review of Anti-infective Therapy, August 2013, 4–22. June 26, 2016. http://dx.doi.org.libproxy.temple.edu/10.1586/14787210.2013.81 4824.

5. White, Bruce A. *PCR Cloning Protocols.* Vol. 67. Totowa, NJ: Humana Press, 1997.

6. Quest Diagnostics, 2013. Web. 24 June 2016.

✓ **Assignment**: Divide your students into groups of 3 or 4. Each group will serve as a Student Peer Review Team for the NHSJS submissions. Ask each group to review this article or other articles that are posted on the NHSJS website. Each group should identify criteria for rating the articles. Have each share the criteria they used and the title of the article they reviewed.

Example 5.8: The Story of the Rift Valley Fever Virus Vaccine

The article on the Rift Valley Fever Virus Vaccine is an example of a well-written, easy-to-read article intended for the general audience of people who may be seeking information from the Centers for Disease Control. Note the limited scientific language, the well-defined subheadings with short explanations, and the use of bullet points for clarity.

Preventing Disease in Humans and Livestock
Centers for Disease Control, October 16, 2016

National Center for Emerging and Zoonotic Infectious Diseases (NCEZID)
In late 1997, a disease outbreak began in East Africa. In three months, 90,000 people became sick and almost 500 people died. Many animals in the region also died, causing economic difficulties for the people who relied on these animals for milk, meat, and as a trading commodity. The loss of human lives and animals was devastating for the communities. The cause of this outbreak was the Rift Valley fever virus.

Rift Valley Fever
Rift Valley fever (RVF) is caused by a virus that is transmitted by mosquitoes. Since it was discovered in 1930, RVF virus has caused multiple outbreaks in Africa and the Middle East. The virus can cause severe disease in both animals and humans. People can be infected from the bite of a mosquito or through direct contact with the blood and tissues of infected animals.

Most people infected with the RVF virus do not have any signs of disease, but some people will become very sick. They can develop blindness, encephalitis (brain swelling), and hemorrhagic fever (unusual bleeding), and some die from the disease. RVF can also cause disease in many species of livestock, such as sheep, goats, cattle, and camels. Many infected animals, especially young animals, die from the disease. Almost all pregnant animals will miscarry if they are infected with the virus.

Monitoring the Environment: Using Satellites to Predict RVF Outbreaks
RVF outbreaks often occur in years of unusually heavy rainfall. These rains cause flooding, which provides a perfect environment for the infected mosquito eggs in the soil to hatch. If health officials knew that heavy rains were coming, they would have time to prevent RVF illnesses in animals and humans.

Researchers have discovered that these heavy rains are caused by changes in ocean temperature which affect weather patterns around the world. Scientists with the National Aeronautics and Space Administration (NASA) can use satellite images to monitor changes in ocean temperature. Health officials can then use this information to predict when outbreaks of RVF are likely to occur and take action to prevent them.

CDC Researchers Work to Control the Disease
RVF is difficult to control because infected mosquito eggs can survive for years in the soil. Infected animals develop high levels of virus in their blood, making it easy for mosquitoes that bite these animals to then become infected with the virus. This chain of transmission must be broken to prevent disease in people and animals.

How do we break the chain of transmission? Vaccinating people is not an option because there is no RVF vaccine. Killing mosquitoes with pesticides is not a good option because it is time-consuming and exposes people to other health risks.

What does work, however, is to vaccinate animals against RVF. By preventing RVF in animals, fewer humans will be infected from mosquitoes carrying the virus or from direct contact with a sick animal. Vaccinations also protect the animals that the people rely on for food and as a source of income.

CDC researchers have developed a *new vaccine against RVF virus for animals*. During early testing, all vaccinated animals were protected against the RVF virus. There were no negative side effects. The vaccine is also inexpensive to produce, and this makes it an affordable option for developing countries.

One Health in Action

When professionals from different disciplines work together to protect the health of people and animals, this is One Health in action. For example:

◆ CDC's development of a new vaccine protecting animals from RVF is a promising development. Public health professionals can now work with animal health professionals to vaccinate animals, and as a result, fewer humans will be infected with RVF.

◆ NASA's use of satellite images to monitor changes in the ocean temperature is providing health officials with vital information they can use to predict when RVF outbreaks are most likely to occur so they can take action to prevent these outbreaks.

By collaborating effectively with individuals from many fields, public health professionals can prevent outbreaks of RVF and better protect the health of people.

Example 5.9:   One Health: Science, Politics, and Zoonotic Disease in Africa

The following report presents the problems of zoonotic disease in Africa and reviews a book on the topic.

Heymann, David L
The Lancet Infectious Diseases, Volume 17, Issue 1, 37

When I first began working as a medical epidemiologist in west Africa during the 1970s, fresh from training in the USA and London, the control of infectious diseases seemed straightforward—vaccines, bednets, handwashing, and condoms were used to prevent infection; antimicrobial, other medicines, and biologicals such as immunoglobulins could be used either as prophylaxis or treatment; and disease was either prevented, decreased in severity, or cured.

It was in Africa, at Yambuku in 1976, during the first outbreak of Ebola, and then a few years later at the newly established Lassa Fever Research Project in Kenema, that what had seemed to me so straightforward and clear was suddenly blurred, complex, and a challenge to understand. By the time that the Centers for Disease Control and Prevention (CDC) team of virologists and epidemiologists arrived at that first Ebola virus disease outbreak and named the virus now known as Ebola virus, the outbreak was already over—fully contained with no further cases. The hospital, which had amplified transmission by the use of improperly sterilised needles and syringes and inadvertently by health workers who tragically became infected treating patients with this highly lethal but previously unknown disease, had been closed. What we later understood as nosocomial amplification of transmission had therefore stopped.

Community transmission had also stopped, and from detailed discussions during the retrospective outbreak investigation, family members of those who had been ill and recovered or died provided further understanding. The conclusion from these discussions, often facilitated by a village chief or elder, was that cultural beliefs had fully contained the outbreak by stopping person-to-person transmission in the community. In fact, communities had rapidly understood that those with Ebola virus disease were to be isolated, avoided, and in some cases abandoned. To their understanding, those with Ebola virus disease had been inhabited by evil spirits that were making them sick by occupying their bodies and at the same time trying to escape to inhabit others who touched or came too close. Once communities understood, they stopped the outbreak.

In Kenema a few years later, working at the newly established CDC Lassa Fever Laboratory with the mammologists who specialised in rodents, the concept of infectious disease emergence in human beings from the animal kingdom became clear. Because Lassa virus disease had no vaccine, and because treatment at that time was ineffective, there was a need to identify and mitigate the risk factors that led to the breech in the species barrier and human infection. And it was the mammologists who provided early understanding of risk factors at the Kenema Lassa laboratory—the significance of the dry season, how this related to grain storage in households and rodents in search of food, and finally how rodents at the time they stole food were contaminating the grain that remained.

But though these social, environmental, and economic factors were being understood in the 1970s, it was not until the 1990s that the concept of emerging infections and human interaction with the environment and ecosystem became common parlance, and with the arrival of the 21st century, the concept of One Health began to weave these factors together under the one health movement.

Kevin Bardosh, in *One Health: Science, Politics and Zoonotic Disease in Africa*, increases the reader's understanding of the One Health movement and its importance in Africa. He brings together the risk factors that result in zoonotic infection by "unpacking how zoonotic disease ecologies and human wellbeing and health are interconnected with wider social, cultural, economic and political dynamics". Through a series of nine case studies—including Ebola and Lassa haemorrhagic fevers—Bardosh and his co-authors provide an in-depth understanding of the various concepts that are linked together in the One Health movement, and demonstrate the importance of a One Health approach in effective prevention and control of emerging and endemic zoonotic infections among both domestic and wild animals. This understanding provides a means to better protect human and animal lives, the environment and its ecosystems, and economies around the world.

The book is a pleasure to read with its detailed and clear case studies, and this is in large part because the co-authors, highly respected in their field, are social scientists who effectively use and describe the research techniques that are often unknown, and sometimes wrongly discounted by those health workers who are working to prevent and control emerging infections. Constant themes are the influence of political economies on zoonotic and emerging infections; the importance of community be it among researchers or those who are a risk; the translation of knowledge and understanding into policy; the need to shift the paradigm of how we deal with these diseases to include not only public health workers, but veterinarians, social scientists, economists, and others in a comprehensive search to understand mitigation or prevent emergence of animal infections in people, and how to more effectively stop their spread if they do emerge and cause human disease. This book is a must read for those who want to learn more about one health in general, and Africa in particular.

✓ **Assignment**: Have students read the above article. Note that the author uses first person. He presents the content in simple, direct English. Ask your students to improve the article by inserting headings to make the content more direct, enabling readers to go immediately to the segments that interest them. The headings should reveal the content.

Example 5.10:   How Machine Learning and Big Data Will Change the Future of Medicine

The following is an example of an article that is too dense; note that there are no subheadings. People doing research want to find information fast. They work from the top down looking for subheadings under which they can find the desired information or explanations.

Gurupreeth Vijay September 23, 2016
NHSJS

Artificial intelligence is fundamentally changing many industries and in the coming decades will transform our society as a whole. However, the most extraordinary developments for all of us could come from machine learning structures used in the medical field. By combining the vast amounts of medical patient data with powerful machine learning data-analytics algorithms, the healthcare sector can save thousands of lives and transition from a static to a dynamic and personalized approach for patient treatment.

Before diving into how machine learning is revolutionizing medicine, it is important to understand what machine learning is, and the sheer quantity and value of the data produced by the medical field. Machine learning is an artificial intelligence based method of data analysis, where an algorithm finds patterns and insights from a given pool of past data that it then applies to new data, primarily to make better decisions and accurate predictions [1]. These algorithms perform best and produce the most high-value predictions when given larger and more diverse training sets of data, and with the recent spike of computing power, this makes them an attractive tool for the healthcare industry [1]. The healthcare industry produces between 1.2 to 2.4 exabytes (1 exabyte = 250 million DVDs of data) every year, which has resulted in a grand stockpile of approximately 159 exabytes of patient data collected from healthcare providers, insurance companies, pharmaceutical companies, and other players [2]. Much of this data is unstructured and unprocessed, but many hospitals are adopting new IT architectures to clean and structure this data for analytics use.

The healthcare sector's troves of Big Data, coupled with technological advances that allow them to create value from that data, has tremendous implications for the patient himself. Medicine is about to become hyper personalized, with patients' medical data being combined with their social media data, financial data, census data, and more to create profiles for each patient that augments their treatment by making it tailored specifically towards them [2]. And at the heart of it all are machine learning algorithms, which reliably and quickly sift through all of this data to help doctors treat you not just based on their experience but also on the experiences of hundreds of thousands of other patients in your situation [2]. Aside from driving medical decisions, these algorithms can, perhaps more significantly, inform doctors of potential health risks their patients might have based on patterns the algorithm has learned to identify from its training data.

The University of Pennsylvania has begun using algorithm based data analytics to improve patient care at Penn Medicine as well as understand different diseases better. Using the machine learning approach, they were able to increase diagnoses of sepsis, a blood infection, from 50% to 85%, and identify such cases 30 hours before septic shock compared to only 2 hours before using past methods [3]. Even earlier this year, Penn Medicine trained a program to analyze how a certain bacterium's genes responded to different conditions. The bacterium, *Pseudomonas aeruginosa*, is highly resistant to most antibiotic treatments, and is present in patients with cystic fibrosis and other lung diseases [4]. The program was presented with 5000 *P. aeruginosa* genes to identify gene expression patterns, and was able to show how the genes responded to different antibiotics, which served as an important start for researchers looking to combat the bacterium and improve treatment for patients with these chronic lung conditions [4].

The healthcare industry has been somewhat slower than other sectors such as finance and retail to adopt artificial intelligence based data-analytics. The University of Pennsylvania is embracing the new technology and seeing extraordinary benefits to their patient care, and while they are setting an example, they are not alone. There have been numerous recent advances which demonstrate the potential of machine learning-enhanced patient care.

A developer of medical algorithms named Zebra has produced two algorithms that when used in unison can identify major cardiovascular problems before they even occur, which they claim can save over 500,000 lives a year [5]. The algorithm based diagnosis is more accurate and cost efficient than technicians' diagnoses, thus capable of dramatically enhancing any hospital's radiology services.

Zebra isn't alone in this regard, either. Google DeepMind has partnered with world leading eye hospital Moorfields Eye Hospital NHS Foundation Trust and created a machine learning algorithm that is currently analysing the information of one million patients to help detect diabetes and age-related macular degeneration (AMD), two conditions that cause sight loss and affect over 100 million people around the world [6]. Early intervention is key in stopping these diseases, which can be difficult to do because human doctors often need a long time to analyze the complex eye scans. Google DeepMind is employing machine learning technology to analyze the scans more quickly and effectively, preventing cases of blindness while also preserving patient confidentiality (all information is anonymous) and collecting data on how to improve future treatment [6].

However, machine learning is proving most effective in the fight against cancer. Mounting an early offense against cancer is a key step of a successful recovery, and a Swiss company named Sophia Genetics has created an incredible solution. It is an AI named Sophia analyzes the genetic code of DNA to diagnose diseases like cancer, and then optimizes that diagnosis by factoring in medical science and expert opinion, allowing doctors to provide the best treatment available to the patient. Sophia also constantly peruses a pool of medical data sent to the company by 170 hospitals around the world, meaning it is always refining its abilities [7]. Even IBM's Watson, while most known for winning the $1 million jackpot on *Jeopardy!*, correctly diagnosed a rare form of leukemia in early August that had been misidentified by human doctors months earlier, saving the life of a 60 year old woman [8].

The other key to an effective recovery from cancer is correctly identifying the type of cancer, which can be difficult as even two very skilled pathologists will only agree approximately 60% of the time when looking at the same slide of tissue [9]. Stanford researchers recently trained a computer program on more than 2000 cancer cell images to accurately identify two types of lung cancer (adenocarcinoma and squamous cell carcinoma) by finding cancer-specific traits and basing its diagnoses off them [9]. Most pathologists can only analyze several hundred traits when making a diagnosis, but the computer was ultimately able to assess more than 10,000 features [9]. The researchers found that as a result, the program was able to distinguish between adenocarcinoma and squamous cell carcinoma more correctly as well as predict patient survival times much better than pathologists. While this approach was applied just for lung cancer, given the computing power and training, a similar program could identify even more kinds of cancer and filter for specific characteristics that only certain rare forms may have.

Vice President Joe Biden recently called for new breakthroughs in treating cancer, and machine learning could be the answer [3]. Hospitals have the data, and machine learning is the answer to using that data most effectively to improve treatment knowledge and patient care. It is important to understand that the technology isn't new, either; the artificial intelligence field has been around since the 1950s but the recent explosion of computing power along with increasing use by various commercial sectors has made many wonder when healthcare will make the full leap as well [1]. True, the field is somewhat caught up in traditional practices and somewhat reluctant to change, but there are other more pressing reasons.

The two major problems stopping healthcare from becoming an interconnected, highly efficient, and highly personalized industry are a lack of uniform data transfers and privacy concerns with patient data. Right now, there is no universally adopted systematic form for the data that hospitals produce, making exchanging and sharing with other facilities difficult. Ideally, however, hospitals should process data in a standardized format which can be transferred and used among all health-care facilities, providing doctors with the most reliable and meaningful aggregate to compare against any patient's case and deliver the most effective treatment [2]. Perhaps the biggest obstacle to the growth of data analytics in healthcare, though, is a concern for privacy from many patients, who are apprehensive about their private medical information being shared even if it is just for researching new solutions and optimizing patient care. Unsurprisingly, this has led many hospitals to adopt new IT security architectures designed to relieve these concerns. Our fundamental need for privacy needs to be balanced with the possibility of enriched patient care for all of us, since the more data that researchers analyze the better the outcome for all of us [2].

Medical applications for AI have been researched for a long time, but it will be quite a while before algorithms are actively aiding doctors in hospitals on a grand scale. Though sluggish to adopt this technology, the healthcare field has already identified how valuable it could be; savings for the industry using data analytics could be as high as $232 billion, and the Big Data analytics sector is already valued at $100 billion and growing at twice the rate of the software business as a whole. However, with the growth of computing power and more discoveries that reveal the power of combining machine learning analytics with healthcare big data, it will not be long before patient health care is forever changed and improved for the better.

Works Cited

1. ""Machine Learning: What It Is and Why It Matters"." *Analytics, Business Intelligence and Data Management*. SAS, n.d. Web. 18 Aug. 2016. <www.sas.com/en_id/insights/analytics/machine-learning.html>
2. Hinssen, Peter, Philippe Gosseye, José Delameilleure, and Hans Vandenberghe, eds. ""The Age of Data-Driven Medicine"." *Data Science Series*. Across Technology, Sept. 2012. Web. 10 Aug. 2016. <http://datascienceseries.com/assets/blog/The_Age_of_Data-Driven_Medicine.pdf>
3. Press, Gil. ""AI and Machine Learning Take Center Stage at Intel Analytics Summit"." *Forbes*. Forbes Magazine, 16 Aug. 2016. Web. 18 Aug. 2016. <www.forbes.com/sites/gilpress/2016/08/16/ai-and-machine-learning-take-center-stage-at-intel-analytics-summit/#76b80aa4108e>
4. ""Powerful Machine-Learning Technique Uncovers Unknown Features of Important Bacterial Pathogen"." *Penn Medicine*. University of Pennsylvania, 20 Jan. 2016. Web. 18 Aug. 2016. <www.uphs.upenn.edu/news/News_Releases/2016/01/greene/>
5. Prabhu, Vijay. ""Can an Algorithm Save 500,000 People a Year? According to Zebra, It Can"." *TechWorm*. TechWorm, 15 Aug. 2016. Web. 18 Aug. 2016. <www.

techworm.net/2016/08/zebra-says-new-machine-learning-algorithm-can-save-500000-lives-year.html>

6. "Announcing DeepMind Health Research Partnership with Moorfields Eye Hospital"." *Health Google DeepMind*. Google DeepMind, 5 July 2016. Web. 18 Aug. 2016. <https://deepmind.com/health.html>

7. Hicks, Jennifer. ""Artificial Intelligence and Data Driven Medicine"." *Forbes*. Forbes Magazine, 27 July 2016. Web. 09 Aug. 2016. <www.forbes.com/sites/jenniferhicks/2016/07/27/artificial-intelligence-and-data-driven-medicine/#47d3b7a95af8>

8. Fingas, Jon. ""IBM's Watson AI Saved a Woman from Leukemia"." *Engadget*. Engadget, 7 Aug. 2016. Web. 09 Aug. 2016. <https://www.engadget.com/2016/08/07/ibms-watson-ai-saved-a-woman-from-leukemia/>

9. Boroyan, Nathan. ""Precision Medicine Study Highlights Role of Machine Learning"." *HealthITAnalytics*. HealthITAnalytics, 18 Aug. 2016. Web. 18 Aug. 2016. <http://healthitanalytics.com/news/precision-medicine-study-highlights-role-of-machine-learning>

 Assignment 1: Ask your students to add supporting headings and sub-headings to the above article, taking out all unnecessary information.

Assignment 2: This is an article that would have wide audience appeal. Ask your students to write a summary of the article for your local newspaper. They can find an example of a good summary in Example 5.3 of this chapter. For the summary, they will need to simplify the article and through the use of a medical dictionary translate the scientific terms.

Example 5.11: First Ebola Virus Vaccine to Protect Human Beings?

Geisbert, Thomas W
The Lancet, Volume 389, Issue 10068, 479–480

Since the discovery of Ebola virus in 1976, researchers have attempted to develop effective vaccines. Early efforts were largely stalled as a result of the small global market for a vaccine for Ebola virus disease because of an absence of financial incentives for pharmaceutical companies. After the attacks in the USA on Sept 11, 2001, several governments invested in Ebola virus because they had concerns that it could be used as a biological weapon. These investments laid the groundwork for several candidate vaccines for Ebola virus disease that showed promise in preclinical studies in animals.[1] Among the most promising vaccines showing protection in the gold standard non-human primate models of Ebola virus disease was a vaccine based on a recombinant vesicular stomatitis virus expressing the Ebola virus glycoprotein (rVSV-ZEBOV).[2] Findings from preclinical studies in non-human primates jointly financed by the Public Health Agency of Canada and the US Defense Threat Reduction Agency showed that the rVSV-ZEBOV vaccine could completely protect non-human primates as a preventive vaccine against all medically relevant species of Ebola virus when given as a single-injection vaccine;[2] and [3] protect 50% of non-human primates against Ebola virus disease when given shortly after exposure; [4] and seemed to be safe in non-human primates as evidenced by an absence of serious adverse events in severely immunocompromised animals [5] and no evidence of neurovirulence in non-human primates. [6]

Outbreaks of Ebola virus disease have occurred sporadically, mostly in central Africa since 1976. These outbreaks have been small in size and generally well contained until December, 2013, when the largest recorded outbreak of Ebola virus disease began in the west African country of Guinea and quickly spread to surrounding countries with cases also being exported to Europe and the USA. As the outbreak grew in magnitude and appeared to be uncontained, efforts to use medical counter-measures to intervene intensified. In an Article published in *The Lancet*, Ana Maria Henao-Restrepo and colleagues follow-up their interim results [7] and present the final results of their ring vaccination cluster-randomised trial in Guinea in 2015 to assess the efficacy of a single intramuscular dose of the rVSV-ZEBOV vaccine in the prevention of laboratory confirmed Ebola virus disease.[8] The study involved vaccinating a ring of all contacts and contacts of contacts of confirmed cases of Ebola virus disease, either immediately or delayed to 21 days after randomisation. Briefly, 2119 contacts and contacts of contacts in 51 clusters randomly allocated, and 1677 contacts and contacts of contacts in 19 non-randomised clusters were immediately vaccinated, and 2041 contacts and contacts of contacts in 47 randomised clusters received a delayed vaccination 21 days after randomisation. Importantly, no cases of Ebola virus disease occurred 10 days or more after randomisation among randomly assigned contacts and contacts of contacts vaccinated in immediate clusters compared with 16 cases in those in delayed clusters. Vaccine efficacy was 100% (95% CI 68·9–100·0, p=0·0045). Vaccine efficacy was also 100% in the non-randomised clusters (95% CI 79·3–100·0, p=0·0033). These data strongly suggest that the rVSV-ZEBOV vaccine was effective in protecting against Ebola virus infection and probably contributed to controlling the 2013–16 outbreak of Ebola virus disease in Guinea.

Protective efficacy is clearly the strength of the study by Henao-Restrepo and colleagues. There have been concerns in the past regarding the safety profile of rVSV-ZEBOV because it is a replication-competent vaccine. In this study, the investigators identified 80 serious adverse events, of which only two were judged to be related to vaccination (one febrile reaction and one anaphylaxis) and one possibly related (influenza-like illness), with all three cases recovering without sequelae. Conflicting safety results have been reported from phase I clinical trials of the rVSV-ZEBOV vaccine with oligoarthritis being reported in 13 of 51 low-dose vaccines in one study.[9] No significant adverse events have been reported in other phase 1 studies.[10] Although rVSV-ZEBOV seems to be highly efficacious and safe in the context of an outbreak, some questions remain. One question that has not been adequately addressed, even in non-clinical studies with any Ebola virus vaccine, is with regard to durability—is the vaccine long-lasting? Is it still protective, for example, 2–3 years after the vaccination? Another question is in regard to improvements in safety: clearly, the VSV-based Ebola virus vaccines appear to be the lead candidates for use in human beings, but can they be further attenuated to reduce the number of adverse events noted in phase 1 trials without reducing efficacy? Results of preclinical studies in non-human primates suggest that this attenuation might be possible. [11]

After 40 years we appear to now have an effective vaccine for Ebola virus disease to build upon. This success has been achieved by leveraging findings from published preclinical studies to justify the use of the rVSV-ZEBOV vaccine during an outbreak without the need for time-consuming and costly good laboratory practices (GLP) or GLP-like preclinical studies required by regulatory policies such as the US FDA Animal Rule, [12] that although well intentioned, are impractical and inefficient in the context of the few high containment biosafety level 4 laboratories that exist worldwide (i.e., laboratories that use the highest level of biosafety precautions and where, in most cases, workers wear positive pressure suits to work the with most hazardous viruses such as Ebola virus).

I have five US patents in the fields of filovirus and antiviral vaccines, including Ebola virus disease, and two provisional US patents: number 7635485, entitled "Method of accelerated vaccination against Ebola viruses" issued to G Nabel, N Sullivan, P Jahrling, and TW Geisbert on Dec 22, 2009, issued to the US government; number 7838658, entitled "siRNA silencing of filovirus gene expression" issued to I MacLachlan, V Sood, LE Hensley, E Kagan, and TW Geisbert on Nov 23, 2010, issued to Tekmira Pharmaceuticals and the US government; number 8017130 entitled "Method of accelerated vaccination against Ebola viruses" issued to G Nabel, N Sullivan, P Jahrling, and TW Geisbert on Sept 13, 2011, issued to US Government; number 8716464, entitled "Compositions and methods for silencing Ebola virus gene expression" issued to TW Geisbert, ACH Lee, M Robbins, V Sood, A Judge, LE Hensley, and I MacLachlan, on May 6, 2014, issued to Tekmira Pharmaceuticals and

US Government; and number 8796013 entitled "Pre- or post-exposure treatment for filovirus or arenavirus infection" issued to TW Geisbert on Aug 5, 2014, issued to Boston University and Profectus Biosciences. I also have two patent provisional US patents: 61/014669 filed Feb 8, 2008, by TW Geisbert pending to Boston University, entitled "Compositions and methods for treating Ebola virus infection", and 61/070748 filed March 25, 2008, by TW Geisbert, JH Connor, and H Ebihara pending to Boston University, entitled "Multivalent vaccine vector for the treatment and inhibition of viral infection.

References

1. A Marzi, H Feldmann. Ebola virus vaccines: an overview of current approaches. *Expert Review of Vaccines*, 13 (2014), pp. 521–553.
2. SM Jones, H Feldmann, U Ströher, *et al.* Live attenuated recombinant vaccine protects non-human primates against Ebola and Marburg viruses. *Nature Medicine*, 11 (2005), pp. 786–790.
3. TW Geisbert, JB Geisbert, A Leung, *et al.* Single-injection vaccine protects nonhuman primates against infection with marburg virus and three species of ebola virus. *Journal of Virology*, 83 (2009), pp. 7296–7304.
4. H Feldmann, SM Jones, KM Daddario-DiCaprio, *et al.* Effective post-exposure treatment of Ebola infection. *PLoS Pathogens*, 3 (2007), p. e2.
5. TW Geisbert, KM Daddario-Dicaprio, MG Lewis, *et al.* Vesicular stomatitis virus-based Ebola vaccine is well-tolerated and protects immunocompromised non-human primates. *PLoS Pathogens*, 4 (2008), p. e1000225.
6. CE Mire, AD Miller, A Carville, *et al.* Recombinant vesicular stomatitis virus vaccine vectors expressing filovirus glycoproteins lack neurovirulence in non-human primates. *PLoS Neglected Tropical Diseases*, 6 (2012), p. e1567.
7. AM Henao-Restrepo, IM Longini, M Egger, *et al.* Efficacy and effectiveness of an rVSV-vectored vaccine expressing Ebola surface glycoprotein: interim results from the Guinea ring vaccination cluster-randomised trial. *Lancet*, 386 (2015), pp. 857–866.
8. AM Henao-Restrepo, A Camacho, IM Longini, *et al.* Efficacy and effectiveness of an rVSV-vectored vaccine in preventing Ebola virus disease expressing Ebola virus surface glycoprotein: final results from the Guinea ring vaccination, open-label, cluster-randomised trial (Ebola Ça Suffit!). *Lancet* (2016), published online Dec 22. http://dx.doi.org.ezproxy.library.tamu.edu/10.1016/S0140-6736(16)32621-6
9. A Huttner, JA Dayer, S Yerly, *et al.* The effect of dose on the safety and immunogenicity of the VSV Ebola candidate vaccine: a randomised double-blind, placebo-controlled phase 1/2 trial. *Lancet Infectious Diseases*, 15 (2015), pp. 1156–1166.

10. JA Regules, JH Beigel, KM Paolino, *et al.* A recombinant vesicular stomatitis virus Ebola vaccine—preliminary report. *New England Journal of Medicine* (2015), published April 1. http://dx.doi.org.ezproxy.library.tamu.edu/10.1056/NEJMoa1414216.

11. CE Mire, D Matassov, JB Geisbert, *et al.* Single-dose attenuated Vesiculovax vaccines protect primates against Ebola Makona virus. *Nature*, 520 (2015), pp. 688–691.

12. US Food and Drug Administration. *Code of Federal Regulations title 21*. https://www.accessdata.fda.gov/scripts/cdrh/cfdocs/cfcfr/CFRSearch.cfm?CFRPart=314&showFR=1&subpartNode=21:5.0.1.1.4.9 (accessed December 12, 2016).

Example 5.12: Multidrug Resistant Tuberculosis: A Continuing Crisis

Burki, Talha
The Lancet Infectious Diseases, Volume 16, Issue 12, 1337–1338

The multidrug resistant tuberculosis epidemic is a crisis. Despite promising new treatments, gaps in funding and political attention are hampering efforts to stem the disease. Talha Burki reports.

On Oct 13, WHO released its 2016 *Global Tuberculosis Report*. It estimated that last year saw 10·4 million new cases of tuberculosis; improved surveillance from India accounted for most of the 800 000 additional cases compared with 2014. 1·8 million people worldwide (including 400 000 people with HIV) are thought to have died from tuberculosis in 2015, and 60% of the disease burden was concentrated in six countries (India, Indonesia, China, Nigeria, Pakistan, and South Africa). WHO urged their member states to sharply scale-up control efforts, particularly in terms of investment.

The report noted that the available funding for low-income and middle-income countries to tackle tuberculosis in 2016 is roughly US$2 billion short of the amount recommended by the Global Plan. A report by Treatment Action Group (*TAG*), released on Oct 25, expanded on this theme, laying bare the extent of the funding crisis in tuberculosis research and development. In 2015, funding in the field stood at around US$621 million, the lowest level since 2008 and a fall of more than $53 million since the previous year; the biggest decline since TAG started monitoring such matters in 2005. The report's authors point out that the 2011–2015 Global Plan had set funding targets for several areas of research and development, none of which were met. The $1·2 billion invested in drug discovery and development over the 5-year period was less than a third of the $3·7 billion envisaged by the Global Plan.

The two reports put together a mixed picture for multidrug resistant (MDR) tuberculosis. WHO continues to describe the epidemic as a crisis, as it has done for the past 3 years. New cases in 2015 held steady at an estimated 480 000. A further 100 000 people are thought to have rifampicin-resistant disease, but not MDR tuberculosis; in May, 2016, WHO recommended that these patients also be treated with second-line drugs. India, China, and Russia accounted for 45% of the combined burden. "Most high-burden countries have already been surveyed and the data on MDR tuberculosis are quite solid", WHO's Mario Raviglione told *The Lancet Infectious Diseases*. "We know where the problem is huge and where it is not."

In 2012, 18% of patients diagnosed with MDR tuberculosis did not immediately start treatment—a situation Raviglione described as unethical. Last year, only 5% of the 132 000 diagnosed patients were awaiting treatment. But that still means that around 80% of people who are in need of second-line drugs for tuberculosis are going untreated. Moreover, the cure rate for MDR tuberculosis is little more than half. "All we can offer people is awful treatment, with a lot of side-effects that are quite hard to handle, and the need to support them through a 2 year course", said Grania Brigden of the International Union Against Tuberculosis and Lung Disease.

Nonetheless, there are some distinctly hopeful signs. "We have reached a critical mass of new drugs", said Mel Spigelman of the TB Alliance (New York, NY, USA). The advent of bedaquiline and delaminid, the first novel tuberculosis drugs to be approved in more than 40 years, in addition to other compounds in clinical development, has opened up possibilities for new MDR tuberculosis regimens. Despite the underfunding, five such regimens have been put into phase 3 trials since 2011, including the 9-month regimen conditionally recommended by WHO early in 2016. The shortened course showed treatment success rates in excess of 80% during clinical trials.

Two ongoing trials, both of which are being conducted by the TB Alliance, have yielded some promising results. Initial data from the Nix-TB trial testing a combination of bedaquiline, pretomanid, and linezolid for extensively drug-resistant (XDR) tuberculosis found that the majority of patients had negative sputum culture at 2 months; the remaining treated patients had all converted sputum by 4 months. Although linezolid is associated with considerable toxicity, the combination is injection-free and thus far seems safe. The cure rate for XDR tuberculosis, which makes up 10% of MDR cases, stood at 28% last year. The NC005 trial tested a regimen of bedaquiline, pretomanid, and pyrazinamide against drug-sensitive tuberculosis, and the same regimen with the addition of moxifloxacin against MDR tuberculosis. Virtually all of the patients with MDR tuberculosis in the phase 2b trial treated with the quadruple drug regimen showed sputum free of tuberculosis bacteria at 2 months.

"Sometime in the next 3–5 years, we should be able to put together a course of treatment for MDR tuberculosis, consisting of oral pills taken once a day for 4–6 months, that is well tolerated, effective, and affordable", affirmed Spigelman. He believes this could push the cure rate to roughly the same as that for drug-sensitive disease (83% according to the WHO report). And if countries are assured that they can provide good treatment, they might be more inclined to scale-up programmes and track down and diagnose the 400 000 or so hidden cases of MDR disease.

Indeed, there have been significant advances in diagnostics over the past few years. Rapid molecular testing can detect resistance at the same time as identifying tuberculosis. The line probe assay recommended by WHO earlier this year tests for resistance to second-line drugs, and hence suitability for the shortened MDR tuberculosis regimen. There is still no point-of-care test, however, and with the notable exception of South Africa, countries have tended to be slow in rolling out the new tools (some places even seem to prefer microscopy). "We have to ensure that we have proper rapid molecular diagnosis everywhere, at the lowest possible level", stressed Raviglione. "It is just a matter of political will."

The 9 month course for MDR tuberculosis costs around $1000 per patient; other regimens cost $2000–5000. Spigelman expects that the prospective new regimen will drive costs down further but exactly how far is difficult to say. Matters may be complicated by the end of the donation agreement for bedaquiline in 2019. However, a market of 132,000 is not large enough to attract multiple manufacturers. Improving detection rates would help, but probably not enough to generate the volume of sales that could cause the price to dip below $100 per dose. For this to happen, a pan-tuberculosis course is necessary.

If the same regimen could be used on drug-sensitive tuberculosis as on MDR tuberculosis, the benefits would be enormous. The market size would be many times larger, for a start, and cover 99% of patients with tuberculosis. Ideally the course would last for around 1 month, so that patients no longer had to take drugs after their symptoms had disappeared. "That kind of regimen would really simplify the programmatic treatment of tuberculosis—it would be a pivotal moment in turning the tide of the epidemic", explains Brigden. But it is a long way from realisation.

There are currently just two candidates in phase 1 trials. "For MDR tuberculosis, we can certainly make some gains in duration of treatment and side-effects, but we are not going to get the ultimate goal of a 1 month or less regimen that works on drug-sensitive and drug-resistant disease", concluded Brigden. She leads the 3P project, a collaborative effort that aims to jump start the production of a pan-tuberculosis regimen by delinking the end price from research and development costs. "Where antimicrobial resistance might be in 25 years, is where we already are with tuberculosis", Brigden stated. "A curable disease, for which we are running out of treatment options, and not attracting anywhere near enough investment—we have to look at new incentives and ways of funding."

Spigelman is optimistic that the next 5–10 years will see greater advances in MDR tuberculosis than the previous 5–10 years. But he concedes that much depends on resources. "As we make more progress, and get towards more success, the amount of money needed to push things over the finishing line is even greater", Spigelman told *The Lancet Infectious Diseases*. "Phase 3 studies and implementation of new regimens are much more expensive than the discovery of new treatments." Nation states and donors will have to be far more generous than they are at present if progress is to be maintained and consolidated. "The clinical trials that need to be done can stretch out over 10 years or they can be done over 3 or 4 years—it all depends on resources", concluded Spigelman.

A cornerstone of the post-2015 tuberculosis strategy is the target to have no families face catastrophic expenditure because of the disease. This implies some kind of universal health coverage and social protection. No small task, and one that will require strong engagement from government departments outside of the ministry of health. But tuberculosis is one of the world's leading infectious killers; if mitigating its ravages is not the responsibility of government, one would have to wonder what is.

✔ **Assignment**: Both Example 5.11 and Example 5.12 are well-written articles on important health issues. Ask your students to identify an audience and prepare a short article or oral presentation on one of those two topics (Ebola or tuberculosis) for that audience.

Science Journal Editorials

Most science journals include an editorial written by the editor or an expert of his/her choosing. The following editorial attempts to persuade scientists to see the writer's approach and then accept it. Here's the plan:

Topic sentence, the purpose of the article, then development of the argument for the editorial.

Supporting sentences that comprise the argument should explain the value and need, even the importance, of the editorial.

The following editorial argues for the inability of scientists to achieve precision control of disease, despite the work that exists by scientists on a plethora of diseases. Editorials usually appear near the beginning of every journal issue.

Example 5.13: Predicting Pandemics

The Lancet, Volume 388, Issue 10063, 2960

"The world is ill prepared to respond to a severe influenza pandemic or to any similarly global, sustained and threatening public-health emergency", concluded an investigation into WHO's response to the 2009 H1N1 pandemic. In 2014, this unpreparedness was again exposed when the Ebola virus struck west Africa and claimed more than 11,000 lives. The continuing Zika virus epidemic highlights that lessons still need to be learned.

Most new epidemic infections are zoonotic, but not all are transmissible between humans. In a study published in *Emerging Infectious Diseases* on Dec 7, Mark Woolhouse and colleagues used virus genome sequencing and mathematical modelling to identify 37 viruses that have already shown some ability to spread between people but have not yet been the cause of an epidemic. Of greatest concern, the researchers suggest, are Middle East respiratory syndrome coronavirus (MERS-CoV), Bundibugyo ebola and Sudan ebola viruses, and several mosquito-borne viruses. Woolhouse and colleagues' shortlist of viruses to watch has also included chikungunya, Zika, and Ebola in recent years, showing the potential of this approach. Although identification of viruses with human transmissibility adds to knowledge of which types of viruses and which circumstances are most likely to cause a pandemic, several emerging pathogens had not previously been seen in humans at all—severe acute respiratory syndrome, for example.

More can be done to predict the next pandemic threat, but when new outbreaks do occur, there remains a need for a better international response. Promisingly, WHO has launched the R&D Blueprint, which aims for rapid activation of research and development activities during epidemics. To be maximally effective, this strategy will need to work within low resource settings, which will require substantial investment and an understanding of the culture of the setting in which it will be implemented.

Undoubtedly, as the authors conclude, the first line of defense against emerging viruses is effective surveillance. But the international community must be prepared to take rapid and effective action if surveillance is to have value—the question remains, have the recent lessons of the Ebola and Zika viruses been learned?

Citations

1. Shi, Pei Yong, and Susan J. Wong. "Serologic Diagnosis of West Nile Virus Infection." Expert Review of Molecular Diagnostics, November 2003, 733–41. June 26, 2016.

2. Hirota Jiro, Shinya Shimizu, and Tomoyuki Shibahara. "Application of West Nile Virus Diagnostic Techniques." Expert Review of Anti-infective Therapy, August 2013, 4–22. June 26, 2016. http://dx.doi.org.libproxy.temple.edu/10.1586/147 87210.2013.814824
3. McVey, D. S., W. C. Wilson, and C. G. Gay. "West Nile Virus." Revue scientifique et technique (International Office of Epizootics), 2015, 431–39. June 26, 2016. Pubmed.
4. "West Nile Virus: Detection with Serologic and Real-time PCR Assays." *Quest Diagnostics*. Quest Diagnostics, 2013. Web. 24 June 2016. www.questdiagnostics. com/testcenter/testguide.action%3Fdc%3DCF_WestNileVirus
5. "WNV Antibody Testing." Centers for Disease Control and Prevention. February 12, 2015. Accessed July 24, 2016. www.cdc.gov/westnile/healthcareproviders/ healthcareproviders-diagnostic.html
6. White, Bruce A. *PCR Cloning Protocols*. Vol. 67. Totowa, NJ: Humana Press, 1997.

Assignment 1: Ask your students to bring in editorials that have been written on scientific topics found in local or large urban newspapers. Do the editorials follow the criteria for a well-written editorial presented in this chapter? Critique and post the editorials on the classroom bulletin board.

Assignment 2: As a class, discuss science-related topics that would make for an informative editorial in your local newspaper. Have groups of students take a topic, research it, and write an editorial. Peer review the editorials and, after revisions, submit for publication in the newspaper. Project-based Learning encourages projects that solve a community problem. Class findings would make a great editorial.

Assignment 3: Assign your students to find examples of editorials in science journals in your school or public library. Ask them to make a copy of one editorial and write an editorial that disagrees with the editorial they found (one, for example, on climate change).

Example 5.14: Veterinary Medicine and Public Health at CDC

Lonnie J. King, DVM
Office of the Director, National Center for Zoonotic, Vector-Borne, and Enteric Diseases (proposed)

Introduction
People readily associate the role of veterinarians with private veterinary practice focused on pets and farm animals, but the true dimensions and contributions of veterinary medicine are much broader and reflect expanding societal needs and contemporary challenges to animal and human health and to the environment [1]. Veterinary medicine has responsibilities in biomedical research; ecosystem management; public health; food and agricultural systems; and care of companion animals, wildlife, exotic animals, and food animals. The expanding role of veterinarians at CDC reflects an appreciation for this variety of contributions.

Veterinarians' educational background in basic biomedical and clinical sciences compare with that of physicians. However, unlike their counterparts in human medicine, veterinarians must be familiar with multiple species, and their training emphasizes comparative medicine. Veterinarians are competent in preventive medicine, population health, parasitology, zoonoses, and epidemiology, which serve them well for careers in public health. The history and tradition of the profession always have focused on protecting and improving both animal health and human health [2].

Veterinary Contributions to Public Health
The veterinary profession contributes to improvement of human and public health by improving agriculture and food systems, advancing biomedical and comparative medical research, preventing and addressing zoonotic diseases, enhancing environmental and ecosystem health, and helping manage 21st-century public health challenges [3],[4].

Bridging Agriculture and Medicine
Since 1892, a total of 14 diseases have been eliminated from equine, poultry, and livestock populations in the United States [5]. The elimination of these livestock diseases, along with outstanding research in animal health, is key to the remarkable gains in the efficiency of U.S. animal production. Partly as a consequence, U.S. residents spend only approximately 10% of their disposable income on food, whereas residents in other countries pay three or four times more [7]. Although this achievement is recognized to have added billions of dollars to other parts of the U.S. economy, its success in allowing the U.S. public access to a nutritious,

affordable, and sustainable food supply—also important for the public's health and well-being—is far less appreciated. The success of the national brucellosis and tuberculosis elimination campaigns has benefited not only the U.S. livestock industries but also human health by substantially reducing these zoonotic threats in animals. Additional public health contributions can be attributed to the Food Safety and Inspection Service of the U.S. Department of Agriculture (USDA), which has substantially reduced the burden of foodborne illnesses, improved food safety, and eliminated other zoonotic threats. Over the years, CDC has worked closely with USDA and the Food and Drug Administration to improve the safety of U.S. foods and reduce antimicrobial resistance in pathogens that infect both humans and animals.

Research

Research in veterinary science is critical to understanding and improving human health [8]. In 1858, Rudolph Virchow, the father of comparative medicine, stated, "Between animal and human medicine there are no dividing lines—nor should there be. The object is different but the experience obtained constitutes the basis of all medicine" [9]. Today comparative and interdisciplinary research is critical to translating scientific advances from one discipline or species to another and providing new insights into human health problems. Scientific fields such as laboratory animal medicine, pathology, and toxicology, when combined with veterinary medicine, have proven especially relevant to success in biomedical research [10].

Zoonoses in Companion Animals

Veterinarians also have contributed to public health through the care of companion animals. Fifty-seven percent of all U.S. households own a dog, cat, or both. In addition, millions of exotic animals, birds, and reptiles are kept as pets [11]. Although pets enrich the lives of humans, they also potentially can threaten public health. Veterinarians help educate the public about prevention of zoonoses; vaccinate large numbers of pets for zoonotic diseases, such as rabies and leptospirosis; and reduce the level of ecoparasites that can transmit human diseases and intestinal worms, such as roundworms and hookworms, which can cause serious health problems in humans. The 60,000 private-practice veterinarians in the United States form a valuable front line for detecting adverse health events, reducing zoonotic diseases, and delivering public health education [7].

Environmental Health

Because veterinarians work at the interface of human, animal, and environmental health, they are uniquely positioned to view this dynamic through the lens of public health impact. Significant changes in land use, expansion of large and intensified animal-production units, and microbial and chemical pollution of land and water sources have created new threats to the health of both animals and humans [12]. Because animals share human environment, food, and water, they are effective sentinels for environmental, human, and public health problems, including bioterrorism.

Concerns are increasing about antimicrobial resistance of pathogens, waste and nutrient management, and potential runoffs into streams, rivers, and oceans. Food animal and wildlife populations are inextricably linked to some environmental problems. Together these have led to creation of a new scientific discipline called ecosystem health, and veterinarians are assuming a leadership role in the field [13].

Contemporary Challenges: Convergence of Animal and Human Health in a New Era

Several decades ago, special factors came together to create a new epidemiologic era characterized by increases in emerging and reemerging zoonoses [14]. Humans, animals, and animal products now move rapidly around the world, and pathogens are adapting, finding new niches, and jumping across species into new hosts. In 2005, approximately 21 billion food animals were produced to help feed a world population of 6.5 billion persons; the United Nations' Food and Agriculture Organization estimates that demand for animal protein will increase by 50% by 2020, especially in developing countries [15].

The lessons learned from severe acute respiratory syndrome, West Nile virus, monkeypox, and avian influenza are reminders of the need to view diseases globally; integrate animal and public health surveillance, epidemiology, and laboratory systems; and create new strategic partnerships among animal, human, and public health professions [16],[17]. Veterinarians are essential to the detection and diagnosis of and response to these threats and are integral to first-line defense and surveillance for bioterrorism agents.

Veterinary Contributions and the Changing Emphasis at CDC

Just as CDC has expanded its role, scope, and influence in public health since its inception in 1946, so has the veterinary profession (D. Satcher, CDC, personal communication, October 21, 1996). Early in the history of CDC, veterinarians in the U.S. Public Health Service and the CDC Veterinary Public Health Division helped reduce zoonotic diseases, especially rabies and foodborne illnesses [18]. Today, 89 veterinarians serve throughout CDC in positions that address not only infectious diseases but also the entire spectrum of public health challenges: environmental health, chronic diseases, human immunodeficiency virus infection and acquired immunodeficiency syndrome, injuries, immunizations, laboratory animal medicine, global health, migration and quarantine, health education, and bioterrorism. Veterinarians contribute as epidemiologists, laboratory scientists, policymakers, researchers, and surveillance experts and in environmental and disease prevention and control programs both domestically and globally.

At CDC, 228 veterinarians have participated in the Epidemic Intelligence Service since 1951 [19]. Forty-one states now have State Veterinary Public Health officials. In 2005, almost 300 students and faculty attended the first veterinary student day at CDC; in April 2007, CDC will co-host an inaugural conference with the Association of Schools of Public Health and Association of American Veterinary Medical Colleges. In addition, CDC has been recognized as a World Association for Animal Health Collaborating Center for Emerging and Re-Emerging Zoonoses. The CDC publication, *Emerging Infectious Diseases*, has highlighted zoonotic diseases in nearly every issue to zoonotic diseases and has devoted an annual issue in each of the previous 2 years. Thus, CDC has provided an important scientific forum for zoonotic disease research and programs both domestically and globally.

The convergence of human and animal health drove creation of the newly proposed National Center for Zoonotic, Vector-Borne, and Enteric Diseases. Plans are being completed to establish several multidisciplinary state-level zoonosis research and development centers. The veterinary profession at CDC has evolved in prominence as a member of the health professions and has established its importance and usefulness to human and public health. Because their education is based on the concept of multiple determinants of health in populations, veterinarians are well suited to help define and achieve the new CDC health protection goals and to continue to contribute to the CDC mission in ways more important, diverse, and profound than ever before.

References

1. Hoblet KM, McCabe AT, Heider L. Veterinarians in population health and public practice: meeting critical national needs. J Vet Med Educ 2003;30:287–94.
2. Schwabe CW. Cattle, priests and progress in medicine. Minneapolis, MN: University of Minnesota Press; 1978.
3. Walsh DA, Murphy FA, Osburn BI, King L, Kelly AM. An agenda for action: veterinary medicine's crucial role in public health and biodefense and the obligation of academic veterinary medicine to respond. J Vet Med Educ 2003;30:92–5.
4. Noah DL, Grayson JK, Caudle LC 3rd. Ten great veterinary public health/preventive medicine achievements in the United States, 1901 to 2000. J Am Vet Med Assoc 2000;217:1834–6.
5. Dunlop RH, Williams DJ. Veterinary medicine: an illustrated history. St. Louis, MO: Mosby; 1996.
6. Steele JH. The history of public health and veterinary public service. J Am Vet Med Assoc 2000;217:1813–21.

7. Committee on Assessing the Nation's Framework for Addressing Animal Diseases, National Research Council. Animal health at the crossroads: preventing, detecting, and diagnosing animal diseases. Washington, DC: National Academies Press; 2005.

8. Committee on the National Needs for Research in Veterinary Science, National Research Council. Critical needs for research in veterinary science. Washington, DC: National Academies Press; 2005.

9. Schwabe CW. Veterinary medicine and human health. 3rd ed. Baltimore, MD: Williams & Wilkins; 1984.

10. Committee on Increasing Veterinary Involvement in Biomedical Research, National Research Council. National need and priorities for veterinarians in biomedical research. Washington, DC: National Academies Press; 2004.

11. Brown JP, Silverman JD. The current and future market for veterinarians and veterinary medical services in the United States. J Am Vet Med Assoc 1999;215:161–83.

12. Zinsstag J, Schelling E, Wyss K, Mahamat MB. Potential of cooperation between human and animal health to strengthen health systems. Lancet 2005; 336: 1242–5.

13. King LJ, ed. Emerging zoonoses and pathogens of public health concern. Sci Tech Rev 2004; 23(2).

14. Smolinski MS, Hamburg MA, Lederberg J, eds. Microbial threats to health: emergence, detection, and response. Washington, DC: National Academies Press; 2003.

15. Delgado C, Rosegrant M, Steinfeld H, Ehui S, Courbois C. Livestock to 2020: the next food revolution. Food, agriculture, and the environment discussion paper 28. Washington, DC: International Food Policy Research Institute; 1999:20–3.

16. Knobler S, Mahmoud A, Lemon S, Mack A, Sivitz L, Oberholtzer K, eds. Learning from SARS: preparing for the next disease outbreak. Workshop summary. Washington, DC: National Academies Press; 2004.

17. Kahn LH. Confronting zoonoses, linking human and veterinary medicine. Emerg Infect Dis 2006;12:556–61.

18. Steele JH, Blackwell MJ, Andres CR. The 50th anniversary of the Veterinary Medical Corps Officers of the U.S. Public Health Service. J Am Vet Med Assoc 1998;212:952–4.

19. Pappioanou M, Garbe PL, Glynn MK, Thacker SB. Veterinarians and public health: the Epidemic Intelligence Service of the Centers for Disease Control and Prevention 1951–2002. J Vet Med Educ 2003;30:383–91.

Afterword

We have come to the end of our journey through *Writing Science Right* together. Now you must guide your students through the labyrinth of scientific and technical writing to ensure their success in writing for their readers, achieving a readable style, and ultimately reporting their research findings in articles and letters and through oral presentations. To help you, we have provided examples, resources, and student assignments, all based on topics that are relevant and current.

Our first focus was on how to help your students become an effective scientific writers. Rule number 1 is know the audience(s) and what they already know about the topic. Unless your students have a clear idea of their readers' knowledge of the topic and their interest level, they have no way to build a report that will achieve their goals with the readers. Chapter 1 provides the basics of writing and the goals writers must achieve: Readers need to understand the writer's meaning exactly in the way it was intended. Science/technical writing requires you to teach your students that no one thinks they really want to read science and technical writing. Help your students determine how much their intended readers know—and don't know—about the topic; equally important, help your students find ways to make the topic appealing so readers are motivated to read it. Many of the articles we have chosen for this book were written to inform readers about the seriousness of global health issues.

Chapter 2 deals with how to achieve a readable style. If your students want their report to be read, they need to use a style that their readers can follow—without having to reread. If readers can't understand a report as they read it and have to reread sentences and paragraphs, they are more likely to disregard it. Paragraphing lies at the heart of effective writing: Begin each paragraph with a topic sentence that summarizes the content to come. Include only information relevant to the topic sentence. Place sentences in a logical order. Use headings to enable readers to follow major ideas. We conclude Chapter 2 with the characteristics of bad and good writing and explain the qualities of a clear sentence. We also emphasize word choice and show the impact of choosing short, clear words instead of long, cumbersome words. Your students should write to express—not to impress. A readable style ensures your students that their ideas will not be lost or ignored.

Chapter 4 deals with the basics of effective oral presentations. We offer examples of well-designed PowerPoint presentations that help audiences follow their points. We also offer guidelines on how to design speeches that will be read aloud, many of which may become part of public or business records and can be used for legal purposes.

How effectively students deliver oral presentations can determine their success. Your students need to know that point! Having them practice giving short, well-designed presentations will ensure that they remember and use the principles that appear in this chapter.

Chapters 3 and 5 include a number of science articles and letters, many taken with permission from *The Lancet*, one of the most prestigious science journals in the world. We have chosen ones that are short and easy to read. Note and point out to your students that all articles have been carefully documented, a process that they must learn to avoid the charge of plagiarism. Articles that focus on health issues offer opportunities for classroom discussions about some of the world's most challenging diseases: antibiotic-resistant tuberculosis, Zika, Ebola, West Nile Virus, Rift Valley Fever, and diabetes. Research on these diseases has become critical, as people and animals cross the world's borders in search of safety and freedom. Our website will feature updated articles on these diseases and will allow teachers to share relevant articles, science letters, editorials and oral presentations on diverse scientific topics.

We trust the knowledge we have presented in this book has given you new insights on scientific and technical writing and has provided you with useful strategies to help your students clearly and effectively communicate their understandings and discoveries. Our fondest hope is that your students will become better thinkers, readers, and writers. Writing is a skill that, with application of the guidelines presented in this book, can enable your students, wherever their careers may take them, to express their ideas with confidence. A world of readers is waiting.